slow
cooking

from around the world

slow
cooking

from around the world

carolyn humphries

foulsham
LONDON • NEW YORK • TORONTO • SYDNEY

foulsham

The Oriel, Thames Valley Court, 183-187 Bath Road,
Slough, Berkshire, SL1 4AA, England

Foulsham books can be found in all good bookshops and direct from
www.foulsham.com

ISBN 978–0–572–03289–0

Cover photograph © Graham Precey, foodanddrinkphotos Ltd

A CIP record for this book is available from the British Library

The moral right of the author has been asserted

**With thanks to Russell Hobbs and Morphy Richards
for providing slow cookers for testing these recipes.**

Printed and bound in the UK by CPI Mackays, Chatham ME5 8TD

CONTENTS

INTRODUCTION

J ust about every country in the world has delicious slow-cooked dishes that bring out the flavour of the food as well as rendering the ingredients meltingly tender. So what better way to enjoy your slow cooker than to create culinary masterpieces from all corners of the globe? Imagine coming in from work to the gorgeous aroma of a sweetly spiced chicken tagine or a glorious, hearty minestrone gently bubbling in the pot.

Today, because the world has become smaller and with ingredients easily imported and exported to and from every continent, fusion food is becoming the norm. Wherever you go, you will see touches of 'foreign' influences on what was once traditional fare. That is all to the good because it means the best from all cultures are blended, creating whole new taste sensations.

Here you will find my favourite slow-cooked dishes from many nations, each with an exciting new twist, using readily available ingredients. You will also get an insight into the different cultures and ingredients of the various countries and regions so you can better understand the ethos of each area's food and become motivated to create your own specialities. Obviously you are going to use your slow cooker most to cook sumptuous soups, chowders, stews and casseroles, but you will also find it invaluable for making dishes you might not associate with a slow cooker, such as terrines, fondue, breads and spare ribs. Most of the recipes are for main courses, but I have included a few speciality desserts and even a tip for making a lovely creamy porridge, cooked overnight to be ready in time for breakfast.

The benefits of the slow cooker are obvious. For the most part, you can prepare the food in the pot, then leave it to cook without having to worry that it will dry out and spoil. Also, because the cooking is so gentle, you can cook on a Low, Medium or High setting, depending on how quickly (or, rather, slowly!) you want the meal ready. To make it easier to follow, I've mostly cooked on High – except for egg and fish dishes, which really do need to be cooked on Low – but you can check the chart on page 13 to vary the heat and cooking times according to when you want to eat. Many dishes can be cooked as one-pot meals: others just require a simple accompaniment such as rice, pasta, couscous, potatoes or just crusty bread and a side salad (which is always suggested in the recipes). The slow cooker also uses far less fuel than a conventional cooker and doesn't steam up the kitchen, even in summer. All the recipes are very easy to prepare using ingredients you should find in any supermarket, and the results are stunning. So embark on this exciting culinary journey right now and enjoy a taste of a different part of the world every day with your new-found cook's best friend.

USING YOUR SLOW COOKER

1   Stand the electric base on a level, heat-resistant surface. Do not use on the floor.

2   Do not preheat your pot unless your manufacturer's instructions tell you to.

3   Put the ingredients in the ceramic crock pot, then put the pot in the base.

4   Add boiling liquid.

5   Cover with the lid and select the cooking temperature (High, Medium or Low).

6   Cook for the recommended time, checking after the shorter time if a range is given. This will usually be sufficient for most cookers but the food won't spoil if it is cooked for the extra time.

7   Taste, stir and re-season, if necessary.

8   Switch off the cooker and remove the crock pot using oven gloves.

COOKING TIPS FOR USING THE SLOW COOKER

- Any of your usual soup, stew or casserole recipes can be cooked in your slow cooker but liquid doesn't evaporate as much as it does when cooking conventionally, so cut down the liquid content by 30–50 per cent (not quite so important for soups) or increase the flour or cornflour (cornstarch) thickener by one-third. You can always add a little extra liquid at the end of cooking, if necessary.
- Should there be too much liquid at the end of cooking, strain it into a saucepan and boil rapidly for several minutes until reduced to the quantity you require, or thicken it with a little flour or cornflour blended with a little water.
- If wanting a brown finish to meat or poultry, fry it quickly in a frying pan before adding to the crock pot.
- For many dishes, it is best to quickly fry onions before adding them – the flavour is completely different from slow-cooking them from raw.
- Make sure all frozen foods are thawed before use.
- Cut root vegetables into small, even-sized pieces and put them towards the bottom of the pot as they will take longer than meat or other vegetables to cook.
- Do not cook too large a joint or bird in the crock pot. It should fit in the pot with at least a 2.5 cm/1 in headspace. If unsure, cut the joint or bird in half before cooking (it will then cook quicker, as when cooking conventionally).
- Most foods can be slow-cooked but pasta (unless pre-cooked) and seafood should be added for the last hour, and cream at the end of cooking. All the recipes in this book tell you how and when to do this.
- Dried beans must be boiled rapidly in a saucepan of water for at least 10 minutes before adding them to your crock pot, to destroy toxins.

- If preparing food the night before you wish to start cooking, store the ingredients in the fridge overnight. Put them in the crock pot in the morning and cover with boiling liquid or sauce before cooking.
- Do not open the lid unnecessarily during cooking as heat will be lost. If you remove it to add extra ingredients or to stir more than once or twice, you may need to add on an extra 10 minutes at the end (but in most cases there is sufficient cooking time built in to allow for this).
- When cooking soups, make sure there is a 5 cm/2 in headspace in the pot to allow for bubbling during cooking.
- When food is cooked, the cooker can be switched off and left for up to 30 minutes. The food will stay piping hot. If you need to leave food keeping hot for longer, switch to Low.
- If you are unsure if a joint of meat or a bird is cooked through, check by inserting a meat thermometer at the end of cooking.
- Most foods can be cooked on High or Low (or Medium if you have it). Fish and egg-based dishes (such as crème brûlée), however, must be cooked on Low.
- If you are planning on being out all day, opt for cooking on Low, then there is little or no chance of the meal ruining even if you are late (particularly if you don't have a programmable slow cooker).
- You can use the crock pot to keep hot drinks such as mulled wine warm, or for hot dips or fondues. Keep the pot on the Low setting.
- Use a crock pot suitable for the quantity of food you want to cook. It should be at least one-third full for best results (but for foods like ribs or chicken wings, a single layer is fine if you have a large pot). Don't use a small pot and pack it all in tightly up to the top or the heat won't be able to penetrate the food – just as when cooking conventionally.

LOOKING AFTER YOUR SLOW COOKER

- Do not put the crock pot or the lid in the oven, freezer or microwave, or on the hob, or under the grill (broiler).
- Do not plunge the hot pot into cold water after cooking or it may crack.
- Do not leave the whole pot soaking in water as the base is unglazed and porous so will absorb the water. You may, however, leave water *in* the pot to soak it before washing.
- Do not preheat the cooker before adding the ingredients (unless your manufacturer's instructions tell you to).
- Do not use the slow cooker to reheat food.
- Do not leave uncooked food in the slow cooker when it is not switched on (so never put it in there overnight ready to switch on in the morning. Store the ingredients in the fridge).
- Do not use abrasive cleaners on the crock pot – but it will be dishwasher safe.
- Do not immerse the electric base in water; simply unplug it and wipe it clean with a damp cloth.

COOKING TIMES

Some crock pots now have three cooking settings but others have only two. I have cooked most foods on High and a few on Low as they will be relevant to all. Use Medium or Low for any of them, if you prefer, and adjust the times according to the chart below. This chart also shows you the approximate conversion times from conventionally cooked soups, stews and casseroles, should you want to try your own recipes (but remember to reduce the liquid by at least a third). Always check your manufacturer's instructions too as their times may vary slightly. The more you use your slow cooker, the more you will become used to the correct times for your own model.

Conventional cooking time	Slow cooking time in hours		
	High	Medium	Low
15–30 minutes	1–2	2–3	4–6
45 minutes–1½ hours	3–4	4–6	6–8
2–4 hours	4–6	6–8	8–12

Quick guide to cooking times

These are, of course, approximate, as the thickness and quality of the ingredient, the amount of liquid and the output of your cooker will all make a difference. As with all gadgets, it is a matter of trial and error!

Main ingredient	Slow cooking time in hours		
	High	Medium	Low
Fish	–	–	1–2
Beef	5–6	6–8	8–10
Lamb	4–5	5–7	7–9
Pork	4–5	5–7	7–9
Chicken	3–4	4–6	6–8
Duck	3–5	4–7	6–9
Turkey	3–5	4–7	6–9
Game birds	3–5	4–7	6–9
Pulses (pre-boiled in a saucepan for 10 minutes)	3–7	5–9	7–10

NOTES ON THE RECIPES

- All ingredients are given in imperial, metric and American measures. Follow one set only in a recipe. American terms are given in brackets.
- The ingredients are listed in the order in which they are used in the recipe.
- All spoon measures are level: 1 tsp=5 ml; 1 tbsp=15 ml.
- Eggs are medium unless otherwise stated.
- Always wash, peel, core and seed, if necessary, fresh produce before use.
- Seasoning is very much a matter of personal taste. Taste the food before serving and adjust to suit your own palate.
- Fresh herbs are great for garnishing and adding flavour. Pots of them are available in all good supermarkets. Keep your favourite ones on the window sill and water them regularly. Jars of ready-prepared herbs, such as coriander (cilantro), and frozen ones – chopped parsley in particular – are also very useful. Don't use dried for garnishing.
- All can and packet sizes are approximate as they vary from brand to brand. For example, if I call for a 400 g/14 oz/large can of tomatoes and yours is a 397 g can – that's fine.
- These recipes were tested in a Morphy Richards 6.5 litre Slow Cooker and a Russell Hobbs Dual Pot Slow Cooker. All models vary slightly so cooking times are approximate.

A TASTE OF
NORTHERN
EUROPE

The Northern European countries, for these culinary purposes, cover a large and diverse area including the British Isles, the Nordic countries, Benelux, Austria, Germany and Switzerland.

What they all have in common is fairly long, cold winters. For this reason, popular foods of the region tend to be hearty and warming – plenty of potatoes, pulses, dumplings, grains, cured and pickled meat and fish, plus a variety of sausages, both dried and fresh. Pork, beef, mutton (more usually lamb nowadays), venison, poultry and game are all widely used. You will also find a large variety of sea and freshwater fish and shellfish.

Cheeses, too, are plentiful and also a wide and varied selection of fresh fruits and vegetables – apples, pears, plums, berries, cabbages, root vegetables and onions being grown throughout. These days there are many influences from the Middle East and Eastern Europe as well as from the Mediterranean, the Far East and, today, North America (especially their fast foods). I decided to choose some more unusual recipes to include here, rather than the ones you may already know, such as Irish stew and Lancashire hot-pot.

This Scottish recipe is traditionally served as a starter on Burns' Night before the haggis. When I was a child I was always confused when that happened because I was convinced this dish came from Wales – I can only assume because it contains leeks! To transform it into a show-stopper, add a tablespoon or two of Scotch whisky to the finished broth before serving.

traditional scottish cock-a-leekie

SERVES 4–6

2 large leeks, thinly sliced
2 chicken portions, skin removed
75 g/3 oz/½ cup pearl barley
1 bouquet garni sachet

1.2 litres/2 pts/5 cups boiling chicken
stock, made with 2 stock cubes
Salt and freshly ground black pepper
8 ready-to-eat prunes, quartered
Chopped parsley, to garnish

1 Put all the ingredients except the prunes in the crock pot. Cover and cook on High for 3–4 hours until the chicken is really tender and the barley is soft.

2 Lift the chicken out of the pot and cut all the meat off the bones. Chop the meat and return it to the pot with the prunes. Cook for a further 30 minutes.

3 Taste and re-season, if necessary. Discard the bouquet garni and serve sprinkled with parsley.

You can use yellow split peas instead of green for this snert, and a small gammon knuckle instead of the bacon and pork if you prefer. Traditionally this soup has a sliced kielbasa (smoked pork ring) added at the end of cooking and is left to cool then reheated the next day to improve the flavour. But I prefer it without, and find slow cooking brings out the full taste.

dutch pea and bacon soup

SERVES 4–6

225 g/8 oz/1⅓ cups green split peas, rinsed
100 g/4 oz smoked or unsmoked bacon pieces
2 belly pork slices, rinded and diced
1 large onion, chopped
1 potato, chopped
1 leek, chopped

1 celery stick, chopped
1 large carrot, chopped
750 ml/1¼ pts/3 cups boiling pork or chicken stock, made with 1 stock cube
A good pinch of grated nutmeg
Salt and freshly ground black pepper
45 ml/3 tbsp chopped fresh parsley

1 Soak the peas in boiling water for 1 hour or in cold water for several hours or overnight. Drain well.

2 Trim any rind, gristle or bone from the bacon and cut the meat into small chunks.

3 Heat a large frying pan, add the bacon and pork and fry gently, stirring, until the fat runs and the meat is turning brown. Remove from the pan with a draining spoon and transfer to the crock pot.

4 Fry the prepared vegetables quickly in the fat for 2 minutes, stirring. Add to the pot with the drained soaked peas.

5 Pour on the boiling stock and add the nutmeg and a sprinkling of salt and pepper.

6 Cover and cook on High for 4–5 hours, by which time the contents should be very soft.

7 Stir well, taste and re-season, if necessary. Ladle into bowls and garnish with the parsley.

I have used half Gruyère and half Cheddar as I find all Gruyère a bit too strong, but this still has all the traditional flavour of Swiss cheese, wine and kirsch. It looks best in a small, round crock pot; if yours is a large oval, you can put the ingredients in a round soufflé or similar dish in the crock pot with some boiling water around it and then continue as below.

swiss gruyère and cheddar fondue

SERVES 4–6

1 garlic clove, halved
15 g/½ oz/1 tbsp butter, cut into pieces
200 ml/7 fl oz/scant 1 cup dry white wine
30 ml/2 tbsp kirsch
225 g/8 oz/2 cups grated Gruyère (Swiss) cheese

225 g/8 oz/2 cups grated Cheddar cheese
30 ml/2 tbsp cornflour (cornstarch)
5 ml/1 tsp English mustard powder
A pinch of grated nutmeg

TO SERVE:
Cubes of French bread or brioche and raw vegetable sticks

1 Rub the garlic clove over the base and half-way up the sides of the crock pot. Put the butter, wine and kirsch into the pot. Cover and cook on High for 20–30 minutes until the butter has melted.

2 Mix the cheeses with the cornflour, mustard and nutmeg and stir into the hot wine mixture. Mix well.

3 Cover and cook on High for 1½ hours, quickly stirring once or twice without taking the lid off for too long, until the fondue is thick and smooth. Turn down to Low.

4 Serve the whole crock pot on the table on the Low setting to keep the fondue hot while you eat.

Variations

You could play around with other types of melting cheese for a fondue.

Try cider or beer instead of wine for a change, with a little splash of vodka in place of the kirsch for the extra kick.

If you can get wild salmon, the flavour and texture is far superior to the farmed variety – and it won't be that bright orangey-red colour either. However, at least having farmed fish means that everyone can enjoy it rather than it being one of the foods only the landed gentry and poachers could enjoy, which is how it used to be!

warm salmon salad with heather honey, lemon and mustard dressing

SERVES 4

1 onion, thinly sliced
1 carrot, sliced
4 thick pieces of salmon fillet, about
    150 g/5 oz each
150 ml/¼ pt/⅔ cup boiling water
1 bay leaf
5 white peppercorns
Salt

FOR THE DRESSING:
15 ml/1 tbsp clear heather honey
10 ml/2 tsp wholegrain mustard
90 ml/6 tbsp sunflower oil

Grated zest and juice of 1 lemon
45 ml/3 tbsp mayonnaise
Freshly ground black pepper

FOR THE SALAD:
100 g/4 oz packet of mixed salad
    leaves
8 cherry tomatoes, halved
5 cm/2 in piece of cucumber, diced
2 spring onions (scallions), chopped
A few chive stalks, to garnish

TO SERVE:
Baby new potatoes

1   Lay the slices of onion and carrot in the crock pot. Lay the fish on top.

2   Add the boiling water, bay leaf, peppercorns and just a tiny a sprinkling of salt. Cover and cook on Low for 1 hour.

3   Meanwhile, whisk together all the dressing ingredients really thoroughly until well blended and glossy.

4   Pile the salad leaves on large plates and scatter the tomatoes, cucumber and spring onions over.

5   When the fish is cooked, carefully lift it out of the pot with a fish slice and lay one fillet on top of each salad.

6   Whisk the dressing again to blend and spoon over the fish. Garnish each plate with a few chive stalks to one side and serve with baby new potatoes.

This is a lovely version of the traditional pot roast. If you would like to have Yorkshire puds with it, buy some ready-made or cook them in your usual way in the oven just before serving. The meat will sit happily in the pot a lot longer – especially if you turn it to (or cook it completely on) Low – but you may find you have to cut it into chunks rather than slices.

slow-roast rib of beef and carrots with sweet mustard relish

SERVES 4

15 g/½ oz/1 tbsp butter
15 ml/1 tbsp sunflower oil
200 g/7 oz Chantenay or other baby
    carrots, topped and tailed
1 kg/2¼ lb rib of beef on the bone
1 bay leaf
2.5 ml/½ tsp dried oregano
Salt and freshly ground black pepper
450 ml/¾ pt/2 cups boiling beef
    stock, made with 1 stock cube
30 ml/2 tbsp plain (all-purpose) flour
60 ml/4 tbsp water

FOR THE RELISH:
120 ml/4 fl oz/½ cup crème fraîche
10 ml/2 tsp made English mustard
15 ml/1 tbsp light soft brown sugar
15 ml/1 tbsp white balsamic
    condiment or wine vinegar
Salt and freshly ground black pepper

TO SERVE:
New potatoes and curly kale or
    another leafy green vegetable

1   Heat the butter and oil in a frying pan. Add the carrots and cook, stirring, for 1 minute. Remove from the pan with a draining spoon and spread out in the base of the crock pot.

2   Add the beef to the pan and brown on both sides. Place on top of the carrots, then add the bay leaf, oregano and a little salt and pepper. Pour the boiling stock over.

3   Cover and cook on High for 4–5 hours. The meat should be very tender but still sliceable.

4   Meanwhile, mix together all the relish ingredients, stirring until the sugar has dissolved. Season to taste, then chill until ready to serve.

5   Transfer the meat and carrots to a carving dish. Keep warm.

6   Blend the flour and water in a small saucepan. Add the stock from the crock pot, stirring all the time. Bring to the boil and cook, stirring, for 2 minutes. Season to taste.

7   Carve the meat and serve with the vegetables, gravy and relish.

This is a version of haricot mutton, which was popular throughout the British Isles in Victorian times. I love using the creamy pale green flageolet instead of the original haricot beans. You could use a bag of economy chops you can buy in large supermarkets, which would make this dish very good value.

rich lamb and kidney hotpot with flageolet

SERVES 4

175 g/6 oz/1 cup dried flageolet beans, soaked in boiling water for at least an hour or in cold water overnight
600 ml/1 pt/2½ cups water
2 onions, chopped
2 lambs' kidneys
700 g/1½ lb best end or middle neck lamb chops
Salt and freshly ground black pepper

15 ml/1 tbsp fresh chopped or 5 ml/ 1 tsp dried rosemary, crushed
1 chicken stock cube
30 ml/2 tbsp redcurrant jelly (clear conserve)
450 g/1 lb potatoes, thinly sliced
25 g/1 oz/2 tbsp butter
50 g/2 oz/1 cup breadcrumbs

TO SERVE:
Spring (collard) greens

1 Drain the beans and place in a saucepan with the measured water. Bring to the boil, part-cover and boil rapidly for 10 minutes. Turn down the heat and simmer gently for 1 hour or until tender.

2 Meanwhile, put the onions in the crock pot. Quarter the kidneys, snipping out the white core with scissors, and place in the pot with the chops. Season well and add the rosemary.

3 Stir the stock cube and redcurrant jelly into the beans until dissolved. Pour the hot stock and beans into the crock pot and arrange the potato slices over the top in a single layer. Cover and cook on High for 5–6 hours until everything is tender.

4 When nearly ready, melt the butter in a frying pan, add the breadcrumbs and fry until crisp and brown. Scatter over the potatoes just before serving to give a crispy topping and serve with spring greens.

This is cooked one day to eat the next so the time factor really doesn't come in to it – you can even cook it overnight. Leave the stock to cool too, then skim off the fat and use it to make soup. The original pickle was made and stored in jars for months; this fresh version will keep in the fridge for a couple of weeks.

old english spiced cold pork with pickled melon

SERVES 4–6

700 g/1½ lb piece of lean belly pork, boned
12 juniper berries
10 ml/2 tsp coarse sea salt
6 black peppercorns
1 garlic clove
100 g/4 oz thawed frozen chopped spinach
A good pinch of ground nutmeg
1 bay leaf
1 slice of lemon
1 clove
300 ml/½ pt/1¼ cups dry cider or apple juice
300 ml/½ pt/1¼ cups water
45 ml/3 tbsp dried breadcrumbs

FOR THE PICKLED MELON:
60 ml/4 tbsp white balsamic condiment
5 ml/1 tsp caster (superfine) sugar
1 sachet of mulled wine spices or 1 piece of cinnamon stick and 1 clove
1 bay leaf
½ small ripe melon, peeled, seeded and diced
3 spring onions (scallions), cut into 2.5 cm/1 in lengths
15 ml/1 tbsp chopped fresh parsley
15 ml/1 tbsp chopped fresh coriander (cilantro)

TO SERVE:
Jacket baked potatoes and a mixed salad

1 Cut the rind off the pork.

2 Crush the juniper berries with the salt, peppercorns and garlic. Spread all over the boned side of the meat. Leave to stand for 2 hours, if possible.

3 Spread the spinach over the spices, sprinkle with the nutmeg and roll up the meat. Tie securely with string.

4 Place the bay leaf, lemon slice and clove in the base of the crock pot. Put the meat on top.

5 Pour the cider or apple juice and water into a saucepan, bring to the boil, then pour round the meat. If necessary, add more boiling water to just cover the meat. Cover and cook on High for 1 hour, then turn down to Low and cook for a further 6–8 hours.

6 Remove the pork from the pot and leave to cool, then roll in the breadcrumbs and chill until ready to serve.

7 Meanwhile, to make the pickle, put the balsamic condiment, sugar, spices and bay leaf in a saucepan and bring to the boil. Add the melon and onions. Bring back to the boil, then remove from the heat and leave to cool slightly. Transfer to a clean jar, cover and leave to cool completely, then chill.

8 When ready to serve, mix the parsley and coriander into the pickle. Slice the pork and serve with the pickle, jacket baked potatoes and a mixed salad.

SLOW COOKER TIP

Rice pudding is deliciously creamy when cooked in the slow cooker. Lightly butter the crock pot. Add 75 g/3 oz/⅓ cup of short-grain rice and 50 g/2 oz/¼ cup of sugar. Bring a can of evaporated milk mixed with a canful of water to the boil in a saucepan. Pour over the rice, stir well, cover and cook on High for 3–4 hours.

This ragout has roots in Wales, England and Scotland, though 'civet' comes from the French cive, meaning 'green onion'. Spring onions or, as here, leeks, are always used to flavour the dish. Originally, a civet was thickened with the blood of the animal. I like this Welsh way of adding a little diced black pudding instead, which gives a delicious depth of flavour.

civet of venison ragout
with chestnuts

SERVES 4

40 g/1½ oz/⅓ cup plain (all-purpose) flour
Salt and freshly ground black pepper
700 g/1½ lb venison, cut into bite-sized pieces
15 g/½ oz/1 tbsp butter
15 ml/1 tbsp sunflower oil
40 g/1½ oz/⅓ cup lardons (diced bacon)
2 leeks, sliced
100 g/4 oz black pudding, diced
100 g/4 oz canned or vacuum-packed cooked, peeled chestnuts

100 g/4 oz whole baby button mushrooms
15 ml/1 tbsp red wine vinegar
150 ml/¼ pt/⅔ cup ruby port
450 ml/¾ pt/2 cups beef stock, made with 1 stock cube
2.5 ml/½ tsp dried mixed herbs
A little chopped fresh parsley, to garnish

TO SERVE:
Creamed parsnips, potatoes and green beans

1 Mix half the flour with a little salt and pepper and use to coat the venison.

2 Heat the butter and oil in a frying pan, add the venison and brown on all sides. Place in the crock pot.

3 Add the lardons to the pan and cook, stirring, until the fat runs. Add the leeks and cook, stirring, for 1 minute. Add to the crock pot with the black pudding, chestnuts and mushrooms.

4 Blend the remaining flour in the pan with the vinegar and port. Stir in the stock and herbs and bring to the boil, stirring. Season to taste. Pour into the crock-pot, cover and cook on High for 5–6 hours.

5 Stir, taste and re-season, if necessary. Sprinkle with parsley and serve with creamed parsnips, potatoes and green beans.

Variation

This is also delicious made with well-hung beef or game birds.

This stew was originally made just with lamb, the cabbage and peppercorns. I wanted to use this as a base, but make an even better dish for our slightly more sophisticated modern palates. Adding the baby onions, potatoes and the piquant relish turns this into a rustic but really sumptuous all-in-one meal.

norwegian peppered lamb and cabbage stew with cucumber and dill relish

SERVES 4–6

60 ml/4 tbsp plain (all-purpose) flour
Salt
10 ml/2 tsp black peppercorns,
  coarsely crushed
4–6 lamb shoulder chops
450 g/1 lb baby potatoes, scrubbed
12 button (pearl) onions, peeled but
  left whole
5 ml/1 tsp pickled capers, chopped
1 small green cabbage, cut into
  chunks and core removed

1 bay leaf
25 g/1 oz/2 tbsp butter, diced
450 ml/¾ pt/2 cups boiling lamb
  stock, made with 1 stock cube

FOR THE RELISH:
¼ cucumber, grated
1 x 142 ml/5 fl oz/small carton of
  soured (dairy sour) cream
15 ml/1 tbsp chopped fresh or
  5 ml/1 tsp dried dill (dill weed)
Salt and freshly ground black pepper

1 Season the flour with a little salt and the crushed peppercorns and use to coat the meat.

2 Put the potatoes, then the onions, then the meat and a sprinkling of capers, then the cabbage in the crock pot, seasoning well with salt. Tuck in the bay leaf and dot with the butter.

3 Pour the boiling stock over, press the cabbage down well, cover and cook on High for 4–5 hours.

4 Meanwhile, to make the relish, squeeze the grated cucumber to remove excess moisture. Mix with the soured cream and dill and season lightly. Chill until ready to serve.

5 Discard the bay leaf from the cooked stew. Taste and re-season, if necessary. Spoon into warm, shallow bowls and serve with the relish.

This is based on an original Irish recipe (of course!). My version uses an attractive buttery filo topping, which is much lighter than the more traditional puff pastry and gives the finished dish a lovely texture. If you don't really care for kidney, you could substitute the same measure of small whole button mushrooms.

steak and kidney crumple-topped pie with guinness

SERVES 4

45 ml/3 tbsp plain (all-purpose) flour
Salt and freshly ground black pepper
700 g/1½ lb stewing beef, diced
225 g/8 oz ox or pork kidney, cut into chunks and core removed
50 g/2 oz/¼ cup butter
2 large onions, thinly sliced
250 ml/8 fl oz/1 cup Guinness

150 ml/¼ pt/⅔ cup beef stock, made with ½ stock cube
1 bouquet garni sachet
4 sheets of filo pastry (paste)
Sprigs of parsley, to garnish

TO SERVE:
Mashed potatoes and a green vegetable

1   Mix the flour with a little salt and pepper and use to coat the beef and kidney.

2   Heat 15 g/½ oz/1 tbsp of the butter in a frying pan, add the onions and fry, stirring, for 3 minutes. Transfer to the crock pot.

3   Add a further 15 g/½ oz/1 tbsp of the butter to the pan, add the meat and fry quickly on all sides to brown. Tip into the pot.

4   Add any remaining flour to the pan, gradually stir in the Guinness and stock and bring to the boil, scraping up any sediment in the pan. Tip over the meat. Stir, tuck in the bouquet garni and season again. Cover and cook on High for 5–6 hours until rich and tender.

5   A short while before the meat will be ready, melt the remaining butter and brush the sheets of filo with a little of it. Fold the sheets in half and brush again. Gently scrunch up each sheet as if crumpling sheets of paper. Place on a buttered baking (cookie) sheet and bake in a preheated oven at 190°C/375°F/gas 5/fan oven 170°C for about 5 minutes or until golden and crisp.

6 Discard the bouquet garni from the casserole, stir, taste and re-season, if necessary. Spoon the rich, thick stew on to warm plates and top each serving with a crisp, crumpled filo sheet. Garnish each plate with a sprig of parsley and serve with mashed potatoes and a green vegetable.

SLOW COOKER TIP

Make your porridge for breakfast in the slow cooker. Mix the ingredients in your usual way and cook on Low overnight.

I first ate schweinebraten, with its wonderfully tender meat, in Austria in 1974. This is the best version I have had since then. You can serve it with potato dumplings or potato pancakes, if you like, but plain boiled or steamed potatoes is less effort. Braised red cabbage (see page 29) is the traditional accompaniment, though I like it best with lightly cooked green cabbage.

marinated pork in buttermilk with fresh sage

SERVES 4–6

700 g/1½ lb piece of boneless pork loin, rind removed
300 ml/½ pt/1¼ cups buttermilk
150 ml/¼ pt/⅔ cup cider or apple juice
30 ml/2 tbsp soy sauce
1 bay leaf
15 ml/1 tbsp fresh chopped sage
Salt and freshly ground black pepper
30 ml/2 tbsp sunflower oil

1 onion, chopped
2 carrots, chopped
2 celery sticks, chopped
30 ml/2 tbsp cornflour (cornstarch)
30 ml/2 tbsp water
5 ml/1 tsp caster (superfine) sugar

TO SERVE:
Plain boiled or steamed potatoes and shredded cabbage

1 Put the meat in a deep dish. Mix the buttermilk with the cider or apple juice and the soy sauce and pour over. Add the bay leaf and sage and some salt and pepper. Cover and leave to marinate in the fridge for 24 hours, turning occasionally.

2 Remove the meat from the marinade and wipe dry. Heat the oil in a frying pan, add the onion, carrots and celery and fry, stirring, for 2 minutes. Transfer to the crock pot with a draining spoon.

3 Transfer the meat to the frying pan and quickly brown all over. Transfer to the pot. Add the marinade, cover and cook on High for 4–5 hours until really tender.

4 Transfer the joint to a carving dish and keep warm. Blend the cornflour with the water in a small saucepan. Strain the cooking juices into the pan, add the sugar and bring to the boil, stirring, until thickened. Taste and re-season, if necessary.

5 Carve the meat in thick slices and serve with the sauce, potatoes and shredded cabbage.

Known as rotkraut, *you could also cook this on top of the stove over a very gentle heat or in a low oven, about 160°C/325°F/gas 3/fan oven 140°C for around 1–1½ hours. Try it with white cabbage too and white wine vinegar, adding a crushed clove of garlic for added oomph. It will keep for several days in the fridge.*

sweet and sour braised red cabbage

SERVES 6–8

1 small red cabbage, shredded
1 onion, thinly sliced
1 eating (dessert) apple, peeled,
  cored and sliced
A large handful of raisins

Salt and freshly ground black pepper
30 ml/2 tbsp light brown sugar
30 ml/2 tbsp red wine vinegar
45 ml/3 tbsp boiling water

1   Mix the cabbage with the onion, apple and raisins, some salt and pepper and the sugar. Transfer to the crock pot.

2   Mix together the vinegar and water and pour over the cabbage mixture. Cover and cook on High for 2–3 hours.

3   Stir and serve.

SLOW COOKER TIP

You can cook your Christmas pudding in the slow cooker, as long as the basin will fit in the pot with at least 2.5 cm/1 in of headroom. Prepare the pudding in your usual way, cover as usual and put in the crock pot with enough boiling water to come half-way up the sides of the basin. Cover and cook on High for 13 hours. To reheat on the day, cook on High for 5 hours.

A TASTE OF
EASTERN EUROPE

Eastern Europe extends a long way and includes very large countries like Russia and tiny ones like Estonia. There are many traditions practised today throughout Eastern Europe that have changed little in thousands of years. They are a mixture of ancient pagan festivals relating to the seasons and farming traditions alongside those of Orthodox Christianity.

The region's people are very hospitable, always giving guests the best food they can produce. At feasts, the host offers up long toasts to honour his guests, while his wife busies herself serving copious dishes and drinks. An abundance of fish has always been prevalent, along with beef and dairy products, wheat, barley and rye, numerous vegetables, mushrooms, fruits and honey. Many traditional dishes are slow-cooked and filling. There are the hearty culinary influences from Germany and Austria to the North and the more exotic cooking styles of Turkey just the other side of the Aegean Sea, with a touch of the Mediterranean from Italy to the west. The people of this region also enjoy plenty of sweetmeats and pancakes, particularly the famous blinis — light yeast pancakes that are eaten in enormous quantities, particularly at the winter festivals, where the golden discs are said to represent the arrival of the spring sunshine after the long, dark winter.

Picking cep mushrooms in Russia to make this marinovannye griby *is akin to truffle hunting in France! Apparently people will go out late at night to a favourite spot just to ensure they are ready to harvest them at dawn. They are often served as a* zakuska, *an appetiser, with vodka. Alternatively, they can be served with potatoes, fried onions and soured cream as a light meal.*

marinated mushrooms in olive oil

SERVES 4

450 g/1 lb cep or button mushrooms
¼ small onion
75 ml/5 tbsp red wine vinegar
75 ml/5 tbsp water
5 black peppercorns
1 clove
A small piece of cinnamon stick

1 bay leaf
5 ml/1 tsp caster (superfine) sugar
2.5 ml/½ tsp salt
60 ml/4 tbsp olive oil

TO SERVE:
Finely chopped onion and a little olive oil

1   Wipe the mushrooms and put in the crockpot. Place all the remaining ingredients except the oil in a saucepan. Bring to the boil and pour over the mushrooms. Cover and cook on High for 2–3 hours.

2   Remove the crock pot from the cooker and place on a heat-resistant board or mat. Leave to cool, then spoon the mushrooms and liquor into a clean screw-topped jar. Pour the oil over and screw on the lid. Store in the fridge for a week before serving to allow the flavours to develop.

3   To serve, lift the mushrooms out of the marinade, discarding the onion, spices and bay leaf, and place on a serving dish. Sprinkle generously with chopped onion, drizzle with a little olive oil and serve.

This delicious bortsch *originated in Russia, although there it is sometimes more of a stew with big pieces of potato, cabbage and, sometimes, beef – but always coloured red from the beetroot. I prefer this lighter version, which was given to me by a Polish friend when we were poor students. It is equally good served chilled.*

beetroot soup
with soured cream

SERVES 4

2 celery sticks, coarsely grated, discarding the strings
2 carrots, coarsely grated
1 small onion, grated
2 fresh beetroot (red beet), grated
30 ml/2 tbsp red wine vinegar

900 ml/1½ pts/3¾ cups boiling beef stock, made with 1½ stock cubes
Salt and freshly ground black pepper
60 ml/4 tbsp soured (dairy sour) cream
2 spring onions (scallions), finely chopped

1 Put the grated vegetables in the crock pot with the vinegar. Pour on the boiling stock and season well. Cover and cook on High for 2–3 hours.

2 Stir well, taste and re-season, if necessary. Ladle into warm bowls and top each with a spoonful of soured cream and a sprinkling of chopped spring onion before serving.

This is a pretty substantial soup – welcoming and warming on cold winter's days. It is often known as military soup, I am told by my son's Polish friend. It is certainly nourishing enough for troops to march on! He says this version is better than the one his mum used to make. You could add some turnip or white radish instead of the celery for a change.

hearty polish
sausage soup

SERVES 4

15 g/½ oz/1 tbsp butter
1 onion, chopped
1 celery stick, chopped
1 carrot, sliced
250 g/9 oz slaska or smoked pork
ring, sliced
¼ small white cabbage, shredded
2 potatoes, peeled and diced
1 bay leaf

2.5 ml/½ tsp dried thyme
15 ml/1 tbsp fresh chopped dill (dill
weed), plus a little extra for
garnishing
10 ml/2 tsp white wine vinegar
1 litre/1¾ pt/4¼ cups boiling beef
stock, made with 2 stock cubes
Salt and freshly ground black pepper

1 Melt the butter in a frying pan. Add the onion, celery and carrot and fry for 2 minutes, stirring.

2 Add the sausage slices and cook for 1 minute, stirring. Tip into the crock pot. Add the fried vegetables and all the remaining ingredients, cover and cook on High for 5–6 hours.

3 Taste, re-season, if necessary, and discard the bay leaf. Ladle into warm bowls, garnish with a little chopped fresh dill and serve.

Herrings and mackerel cooked in this way make a delicious appetiser or light lunch. There are variations throughout this region and Northern Europe. In Britain this method of pickling fish is called sousing. In Scandinavia this sort of pickled fish is usually served as part of a smörgåsbord.

rollmops
with fresh dill

SERVES 4

4 small herring or mackerel,
   cleaned, heads and tails removed
Salt and freshly ground black pepper
2 small onions, thinly sliced
8 small sprigs of dill (dill weed)
300 ml/½ pt/1¼ cups distilled white
   vinegar
300 ml/½ pt/1¼ cups water

15 ml/1 tbsp caster (superfine)
   sugar
1 bay leaf

TO SERVE:
A warm potato salad, dressed with
   soured (dairy sour) cream, and a
   large green salad

1 Slit the fish down to the tail and open up. Lay the fish one at a time on a board, skin-side up. Run your thumb firmly down the centre of the fish several times, from the head end to the tail. Turn the fish over, carefully remove the backbone and any loose bones and trim off the fins. Cut the fillets in halves lengthways.

2 Sprinkle the fillets with salt and pepper and lay a few of the onion slices and a sprig of dill on each. Roll up from the head end.

3 Place the fish in the crock pot, tail-ends down, and scatter the rest of the onion over. Put the vinegar, water and sugar in a saucepan and bring to the boil, stirring to dissolve the sugar. Pour over the fish, add the bay leaf, cover and cook on Low for 1–2 hours until cooked through.

4 Transfer the rollmops to a container with a sealable lid and pour the cooking liquid over. Leave to cool, then cover and chill. To eat, drain well and serve cold with warm potato salad dressed with soured cream and a large green salad.

Variation

You could also serve this with the traditional Polish and Russian accompaniments of soured cream and more onions and potatoes.

Rindergulasch is a Hungarian speciality of which there are thousands of variations. Beef, paprika and soured cream are the staples – the other flavourings vary from cook to cook. Some make it a plain beef stew, with potatoes and carrots served separately, but I prefer them thrown in for the extra flavour and texture they give.

seeded beef and vegetable goulash

SERVES 4

60 ml/4 tbsp plain (all-purpose) flour
Salt and freshly ground black pepper
700 g/1½ lb braising steak, trimmed
   and cubed
45 ml/3 tbsp sunflower or olive oil
2 onions, peeled and sliced
1 garlic clove, crushed
2 large carrots, diced
3 large potatoes, diced
2 green (bell) peppers, seeded and
   sliced

15 ml/1 tbsp paprika
600 ml/1 pt/2½ cups beef stock,
   made with 1 stock cube
30 ml/2 tbsp tomato purée (paste)
5 ml/1 tsp caster (superfine) sugar
60 ml/4 tbsp soured (dairy sour)
   cream
5 ml/1 tsp caraway seeds
5 ml/1 tsp poppy seeds

TO SERVE:
Coarse rye bread

1 Mix the flour with a little salt and pepper and use to coat the beef.

2 Heat half the oil in a frying pan. Add the prepared vegetables and cook, stirring, for 2 minutes. Transfer to the crock pot.

3 Heat the remaining oil in the pan, add the beef and cook, stirring, until it is browned on all sides. Add to the crock pot.

4 Stir the paprika, stock, tomato purée and sugar into the pan and bring to the boil, scraping up any meat residues from the pan. Pour over the beef. Cover and cook on High for 5–6 hours.

5 Stir well, taste and re-season, if necessary. Ladle into warm bowls and top with a spoonful of soured cream and a sprinkling of caraway and poppy seeds. Serve with coarse rye bread.

This rich, creamy Hungarian dish is also good made with chicken or beef. Use sweet or hot paprika, whichever you prefer – I like the sweet one for this dish but you may want something with a bit more bite. If you like sauerkraut, try serving it hot, sprinkled with caraway seeds, instead of the green salad.

creamy paprika pork with pimientos

SERVES 4

15 ml/1 tbsp sunflower oil
1 large onion, chopped
700 g/1½ lb diced pork
15 ml/1 tbsp paprika
45 ml/3 tbsp plain (all-purpose) flour
300 ml/½ pt/1¼ cups chicken stock, made with 1 stock cube
200 g/7 oz/1 small can of pimientos, drained and cut into strips
Salt and freshly ground black pepper
5 ml/1 tsp caster (superfine) sugar
150 ml/¼ pt/⅔ cup soured (dairy sour) cream
15 ml/1 tbsp chopped fresh parsley, to garnish

TO SERVE:
Noodles and a green salad

1   Heat the oil in a saucepan over a high heat, add the onion and pork and brown, stirring, for 3 minutes.

2   Add the paprika and flour and cook for 1 minute. Blend in the stock and bring to the boil, stirring. Tip into the crock pot.

3   Add the pimientos, a little salt and pepper and the sugar. Cover and cook on High for 3–4 hours.

4   Stir in the soured cream, taste and re-season, if necessary. Serve garnished with parsley on a bed of noodles, with a green salad.

I first had this in the hills near Podgora in Yugoslavia (now Croatia) in the late 1970s. It is gloriously simple to make but packed with flavour. It is traditionally cooked in a large, shallow earthenware pot and served with finely shredded white cabbage, tossed in red wine vinegar, olive oil and lots of black pepper.

three-meat casserole with herbs and potatoes

SERVES 4

60 ml/4 tbsp olive oil
4 small chicken portions
4 pork chops
4 lamb chops
8 potatoes, peeled and cut into large wedges
2 garlic cloves, crushed

2 large sprigs of rosemary
1 large bay leaf
250 ml/8 fl oz/1 cup boiling chicken stock, made with 1 stock cube
Salt and freshly ground black pepper
45 ml/3 tbsp chopped fresh parsley

1 Heat the oil in a large frying pan. Add the meats in batches and fry to brown.

2 Arrange the potatoes in the base of the crock pot and place the meat on top. Add the garlic, rosemary and bay leaf, pour the stock over and season well. Cover and cook on High for 3–5 hours (depending on the thickness of the chops).

3 Taste and re-season, if necessary, and sprinkle with the parsley before serving.

SLOW COOKER TIP

Your crock pot can make mulled wine and hot punches. Use your usual recipes, cover and heat on High until piping hot, then turn down the setting to Low to keep it at the right temperature.

This dish, sarmale, originates from Romania, but you can find versions of it all over the world. I particularly like this one as the mixture of meats gives a wonderful flavour. You will need to choose a large cabbage so you have plenty of big outer leaves for the rolls. Use the rest of it shredded as a vegetable the following day.

braised stuffed cabbage rolls with caraway

SERVE 4

8 large cabbage leaves
2 spring onions (scallions), finely
  chopped
1 garlic clove, crushed
100 g/4 oz/½ cup long-grain rice
100 g/4 oz minced (ground) beef
100 g/4 oz minced pork
10 ml/2 tsp paprika
2.5 ml/½ tsp hot paprika or chilli
  powder

Salt and freshly ground black pepper
15 ml/1 tbsp caraway seeds
1 smoked pork ring, sliced
600 ml/1 pt/2½ cups boiling beef
  stock, made with 1 stock cube
1 bay leaf

TO SERVE:
Plain boiled potatoes and mustard

1 Cut the thick central stalk out of the base of each cabbage leaf. Bring a pan of water to the boil, drop in the leaves and boil for 2 minutes. Drain, rinse with cold water and drain again.

2 Mix together all the remaining ingredients except the pork ring, stock and bay leaf.

3 Divide the mixture between the cabbage leaves. Overlap the edges where the stalk has been removed, then fold in the sides and roll up to form parcels. Pack into the crock pot with the folds downwards.

4 Tuck the pork ring slices in between the rolls, pour the boiling stock over and add the bay leaf. Cover and cook on High 3–4 hours until tender.

5 Discard the bay leaf. Strain off the cooking liquid into a saucepan and boil rapidly until reduced by half. Taste and re-season, if necessary.

6 Transfer the cabbage rolls to warm plates and spoon the juices over. Serve with potatoes and mustard.

This dish was invented in Russia in the late nineteenth century in
St Petersburg by the chef to the Russian general Count Pavel Stroganov.
It is basically beef with mushrooms and onions in a soured cream sauce.
Some recipes use fillet steak and stir-fry it quickly. I prefer this slow-
cooked version, which has much more flavour.

russian beef stroganov
laced with brandy

SERVES 4

75 ml/5 tbsp plain (all-purpose) flour
5 ml/1 tsp English mustard powder
Salt and freshly ground black pepper
700 g/1½ lb braising steak, cut into
   short fingers
50 g/2 oz/¼ cup butter
1 large onion, halved and thinly
   sliced
100 g/4 oz button mushrooms,
   sliced

1 x 415 g/14½ oz/large can of beef
   consommé
150 ml/¼ pt/⅔ cup dry white wine
15 ml/1 tbsp brandy
120 ml/4 fl oz/½ cup soured (dairy
   sour) cream
15 ml/1 tbsp chopped fresh parsley

TO SERVE:
Plain boiled rice and a beetroot
   salad

1 Mix the flour with the mustard and a little salt and pepper. Use to coat the meat.

2 Heat half the butter in a frying pan. Add the onion and mushrooms and fry, stirring, for 2 minutes. Transfer to the crock pot with a draining spoon.

3 Heat the remaining butter in the frying pan. Add the beef and cook quickly, stirring, until browned all over. Add to the pot.

4 Add any remaining flour to the pan and stir in the consommé and wine. Bring to the boil, stirring, then pour over the beef and stir well. Add the brandy. Cover and cook on High for 5–6 hours.

5 Stir in the soured cream, taste and re-season, if necessary. Serve garnished with the parsley on a bed of rice, with a beetroot salad.

This stew, known as bigos, *was originally made with hunted meats such as rabbits, game birds and venison and was cooked one day, then kept for several days to improve the flavour. You could make it the traditional way with half sauerkraut and half sweet cabbage (make sure you rinse the sauerkraut well first) but I just love it made with all sweet cabbage.*

polish hunters' stew
with pork, chicken and vegetables

SERVES 4

25 g/1 oz/2 tbsp butter
100 g/4 oz lardons (diced bacon)
225 g/8 oz diced pork
2–3 skinless chicken breasts, cubed
2 onions, cut into chunks
2 garlic cloves, crushed
100 g/4 oz cep or button
  mushrooms, sliced
½ small green cabbage, finely
  shredded
2 eating (dessert) apples, peeled,
  cored and sliced

1 smoked pork ring, sliced
400 g/14 oz/1 large can of chopped
  tomatoes
400 ml/14 fl oz/1¾ cups chicken
  stock, made with 1 stock cube
1 bay leaf
Salt and freshly ground black pepper

TO SERVE:
Soured (dairy sour) cream, dark rye
  bread and plain boiled potatoes

1 Melt the butter in a frying pan, add the lardons, pork and chicken and brown all over. Transfer to the crock pot with a draining spoon.

2 Add the onions, garlic and mushrooms to the frying pan and fry quickly for 2 minutes, stirring. Tip into the pot.

3 Add the cabbage, apple slices and pork ring slices to the pot and mix well.

4 Tip the tomatoes and stock into the frying pan. Bring to the boil, then pour into the pot. Tuck in the bay leaf and season well. Cover and cook on High for 3–4 hours until the meats are really tender and the cabbage is soft.

5 Discard the bay leaf. Stir, taste and re-season, if necessary. Ladle into warm bowls and serve with soured cream, rye bread and potatoes.

This Czechoslovakian steamed bread, called knedliky, *is served everywhere as an alternative to potatoes, rice or pasta. It is cooked in a roll, traditionally in a pudding cloth, then cut with a wire or strong thread into slices because using a knife would squash it. You can experiment with a cheese wire, if you have one.*

czechoslovakian steamed white bread roll

MAKES 1 MEDIUM LOAF

250 ml/8 fl oz/1 cup milk
300 g/11 oz/2¾ cups plain (all-purpose) flour
5 ml/1 tsp easy-blend dried yeast

1.5 ml/¼ tsp salt
2.5 ml/½ tsp sugar
1 egg

1 Heat the milk to hand-hot.

2 Tip into a food processor with the dough hook fitted and add all the remaining ingredients. Run the machine until a smooth dough has formed. Continue to run the machine for 1 minute to knead the dough.

3 Roll the dough into a thick sausage and place on a sheet of non-stick baking parchment inside a large sheet of foil. Wrap loosely, allowing room for the dough to rise, and seal the top and ends well. Wrap in a second sheet of foil, sealing it to make sure water cannot get in. Leave in a warm place for 45 minutes to rise.

4 Half-fill the slow cooker with boiling water and switch to High. Add the roll to the water, cover and cook on High for 2–3 hours.

5 Carefully remove the knedliky from the slow cooker. Unwrap and tip on to a board with a piece of thread laid across it towards one end. Lift up each end of the thread and cross it over the top of the bread, then pull to cut a slice. Move the thread along and slice again. Repeat until all the roll is sliced. Keep the cut slices warm on a plate covered with kitchen paper (paper towel) over a pan of simmering water until ready to eat.

A TASTE OF THE
MEDITERRANEAN

Olive groves, vineyards, ripe tomatoes, sun, sea and fishing boats – a picture of the Mediterranean can be painted with just those few words. Actually, these days it isn't quite like that; the sea is so overfished that much of the seafood has to be imported. However, the traditional fish and shellfish dishes endure, using local produce when available but, if not, from wherever they can get it! For the purposes of this book I have included recipes from France, Italy, Spain and Greece in this section. I know that, technically speaking, parts of France and Spain are not on the Med, but I can't start splitting countries!

The foods from this region are probably some of the most well-known and popular in the world. The aubergines and artichokes, peppers and courgettes, garlic and onions from the fields; the rustic dried beans, breads and preserved sausages and meats from the hills and mountains; the fresh meat and poultry, fragrant herbs and a sprinkling of sweet spices; cheeses from cows, sheep, goats and buffalo; plus a colourful array of fresh soft, vine and citrus fruits and, of course, olives. With all these you have an almost perfect collection of ingredients that lend themselves to both hearty peasant food and the elegant dining of the rich and famous.

As with many of the recipes in this book, minestrone has so many variations you could ring the changes hundreds of times! You can add diced bacon, and use potatoes or lentils instead of haricot beans and rice instead of pasta. I sometimes add a small handful of freshly torn basil leaves just before serving.

traditional italian minestrone

SERVES 4–6

15 ml/1 tbsp olive oil
1 large onion, halved and thinly
    sliced
1 garlic clove, crushed
2 carrots, finely chopped
1 turnip, finely chopped
1 celery stick, finely chopped
400 g/14 oz/1 large can of chopped
    tomatoes

1 bay leaf
10 ml/2 tsp vegetable stock powder
425 g/15 oz/1 large can of haricot
    (navy) beans, drained
¼ small green cabbage, shredded
Salt and freshly ground black pepper
50 g/2 oz short-cut macaroni

TO SERVE:
Freshly grated Parmesan cheese

1 Melt the oil in a frying pan. Add the onion, garlic, carrots, turnip and celery and fry for 2 minutes, stirring. Tip into the crock pot.

2 Stir in the tomatoes. Fill the can twice with boiling water and add to the pot. Add the bay leaf, stock powder, beans, cabbage and seasoning to taste. Cover and cook on High for 3–4 hours.

3 Remove the lid, stir in the macaroni and quickly re-cover the pot. Cook for a further 45 minutes.

4 When cooked, discard the bay leaf, taste and re-season, if necessary. Ladle into warm bowls and serve with grated Parmesan cheese.

This dish is said to have been made first with goose and pork fat for the famous 17th century French gourmand, François Rabelais. Pork is now the more usual meat used. A French cook would always make at least double the quantity because it keeps for so long. When you've tried it and like it, I suggest you do the same!

pork rillettes
with rosemary

SERVES 4–6

500 g/18 oz fat belly pork
1 large garlic clove, crushed
7.5 ml/1½ tsp coarse sea salt
A sprig of rosemary
1 bay leaf

1 clove
Freshly ground black pepper
45 ml/3 tbsp boiling water
25 g/1 oz/2 tbsp lard (shortening)

1 Cut off any bones and rind from the pork. Lay the meat in the crock pot with the bones and rind alongside.

2 Add all the remaining ingredients except the lard. Cover and cook on High for 5–6 hours.

3 Discard the herbs, clove, bones and rind. Tip the meat and juices into a sieve (strainer) over a bowl. Cover and leave to drain and cool. Chill the liquid so the fat solidifies.

4 Tip the meat on to a board and, using two forks, shred the meat, then pack it into a clean jar.

5 Scoop the fat off the cooking juices and pour any juices into the rillettes. Melt the fat with the lard and pour over the top of the meat. Cover the jar with a lid and store in the fridge for up to 1 month. Once the jar is opened, eat within 2 days.

This rich pâté comes from the Perigord region of France. It is sometimes flavoured with the truffles for which that area is famous. Traditionally it is cooked with a split pig's trotter on the top to give a jellied glaze, but they can be hard to come by these days so I've used some powdered gelatine instead.

country pork liver pâté

SERVES 6–8

9 rashers (slices) of streaky bacon, rinded
1 onion, quartered
2 garlic cloves
A small handful of fresh parsley
8 fresh sage leaves or 2.5 ml/½ tsp dried sage
350 g/12 oz belly pork, skinned
100 g/4 oz smoked bacon pieces, trimmed of any rind or gristle
450 g/1 lb pigs' liver

6 juniper berries, crushed
1.5 ml/¼ tsp ground nutmeg
A good pinch of ground cloves
60 ml/4 tbsp red wine
30 ml/2 tbsp brandy
10 ml/2 tsp salt
Freshly ground black pepper
1 bay leaf
2 slices of orange
10 ml/2 tsp powdered gelatine

1 Line a 1.5 litre/2½ pt/6 cup terrine or similar dish with some of the bacon rashers, trimming to fit as necessary.

2 Using a food processor or mincer (grinder), process the onion, garlic, herbs, pork, bacon and liver.

3 Mix in the spices, wine, brandy, salt and a good grinding of pepper. Turn into the prepared dish and level the surface.

4 Top with the remaining bacon, then arrange the bay leaf and orange slices on top. Cover with a lid or foil and put in the crock pot. Add enough boiling water to come half-way up the sides of the dish. Cover and cook on High for 5–6 hours.

5 Remove the dish from the crock pot and take off the lid or foil. Pour off the liquid into a bowl and stir in the gelatine until dissolved (if necessary, stand the bowl in a pan of gently simmering water or heat very briefly in the microwave but do not allow to boil). Pour over the terrine again, then re-cover with the lid or fresh foil. Leave until cold, then chill in the fridge. The pâté improves with keeping for several days before eating.

The first time I ate this was at a restaurant in Venice but it just contained clams and prawns. I love my version with squid, mussels and scallops. This is a dish that doesn't sit well after cooking as the pasta will go soggy. If you know you won't be ready to eat it straight away, turn off the cooker 10 minutes after adding the seafood. It will be fine for up to an hour.

macaroni with squid, mussels and scallops

SERVES 4

30 ml/2 tbsp olive oil
1 large onion, chopped
1 garlic clove, crushed
350 g/12 oz short-cut macaroni
1 litre/1¾ pts/4¼ cups chicken
   stock, made with 2 stock cubes
A few saffron strands
2.5 ml/½ tsp dried oregano
Salt and freshly ground black pepper
1 bay leaf

100 g/4 oz/1 cup thawed frozen
   peas
400 g/14 oz raw seafood cocktail,
   thawed if frozen
30 ml/2 tbsp fresh chopped parsley
Wedges of lemon, to garnish

TO SERVE:
Ciabatta bread and a green salad

1   Heat the oil in a frying pan. Add the onion and garlic and fry, stirring, for 2 minutes. Add the macaroni and toss in the oil to coat.

2   Add the stock, saffron, oregano and a little salt and pepper. Bring to the boil and tip into the crock pot. Add the bay leaf. Cover and cook on High for 30 minutes.

3   Add the peas and seafood, stir and cook for a further 30 minutes until cooked through and the pasta is just tender and most of the liquid has been absorbed.

4   Stir, taste and re-season, if necessary. Discard the bay leaf, sprinkle with the parsley, garnish with lemon wedges and serve with ciabatta bread and a green salad.

This is, basically, beef cooked in red wine but that doesn't begin to describe the flavour of the finished dish. As it is such a favourite, I had to include it, but don't be tempted to use an inferior burgundy! Coq au Vin (chicken in wine) is almost identical; just substitute chicken portions for the beef, and chicken stock for beef stock and cook on High for 3–4 hours.

beef in burgundy
with button mushrooms and onions

SERVES 4

60 ml/4 tbsp plain flour
Salt and freshly ground black pepper
700 g/1½ lb diced braising steak
45 ml/3 tbsp sunflower oil
50 g/2 oz lardons (diced bacon)
2 carrots, sliced
12 button (pearl) onions, peeled but
    left whole
100 g/4 oz whole button
    mushrooms

300 ml/½ pt/1¼ cups burgundy
200 ml/7 fl oz/scant 1 cup beef
    stock, made with 1 stock cube
15 ml/1 tbsp brandy
15 ml/1 tbsp tomato purée (paste)
2.5 ml/½ tsp Dijon mustard
5 ml/1 tsp caster (superfine) sugar
1 bouquet garni sachet

TO SERVE:
French bread and a green salad

1 Mix the flour with a little salt and pepper in a plastic bag. Add the meat and shake the bag thoroughly to coat the meat in the flour.

2 Heat 15 ml/1 tbsp of the oil in a frying pan, add the lardons and carrots and fry for 2 minutes, stirring. Remove from the pan with a draining spoon and place in the crock pot.

3 Add the onions to the frying pan. Brown lightly, remove from the pan and reserve.

4 Add the remaining oil to the frying pan. Tip in the meat and brown on all sides. Transfer to the crock pot and add the onions and mushrooms.

5 Add any remaining flour to the frying pan, then blend in the wine, stock, brandy, tomato purée, mustard and sugar. Season well. Bring to the boil and pour into the crock pot. Add the bouquet garni. Cover and cook on High for 5–6 hours until the meat is really tender and bathed in a rich sauce.

6 Discard the bouquet garni, taste and re-season, if necessary. Serve with French bread and a green salad.

This is a delicious and unusual Spanish recipe, known as cordoniz en escabeche de modena. Some say it comes from the north of the country, but others claim it comes from Madrid. It is sometimes served with just a plain fruit purée but I prefer the fragrant mix of parsnips and pears, which go so well with the walnut-flavoured dressing.

quail in balsamic and walnut dressing with pear and parsnip purée

SERVES 4

4 or 8 quail (4 for small appetites,
   8 for larger ones)
Salt and freshly ground black pepper
30 ml/2 tbsp olive oil
30 ml/2 tbsp balsamic condiment
1 garlic clove, crushed
150 ml/¼ pt/⅔ cup beef stock, made
   with ½ stock cube
A good handful of fresh parsley
50 g/2 oz/½ cup walnut pieces
90 ml/6 tbsp sunflower oil

FOR THE PURÉE:
2 large parsnips, cut into chunks
3 ripe pears, peeled, cored and
   chopped
A good knob of unsalted (sweet)
   butter
Salt and freshly ground black pepper
Sprigs of parsley, to garnish

TO SERVE:
Steamed courgettes

1   Spatchcock the quail: split them down either side of the backbone, remove the backbone then open the birds out flat. Wash them well under cold water and pat dry on kitchen paper (paper towel). Season lightly.

2   Heat the olive oil in a frying pan. Add the birds and brown on both sides. Transfer to the crock pot.

3   Stir the vinegar, garlic and stock into the frying pan. Bring to the boil and pour over the birds. Cover and cook on High for 2–3 hours.

4   Meanwhile, put the parsley and nuts in a blender with a little salt and pepper. Run the machine and trickle in the sunflower oil to form an oily paste, stopping and scraping down the sides as necessary.

5 To make the purée, about 20 minutes before the birds will be ready cook the parsnips in boiling, lightly salted water until tender. Drain, add the pears and mash thoroughly with the butter. Season lightly.

6 Lift the quail out of the crock pot and stir the walnut mixture into the cooking juices. Return the quail to the pot, cover and leave for 5 minutes.

7 Spoon the pear and parsnip purée on to four warm plates. Top each with one or two quail and spoon the walnut dressing over. Garnish with sprigs of parsley and serve with steamed courgettes.

SLOW COOKER TIP

You can cook lasagne in your slow cooker. Make your usual recipe, ensuring that the white sauce is quite thick. Layer the meat, lasagne sheets and sauce in the centre of the pot (it doesn't matter the pot is bigger than the layers), finishing with a layer of pasta, then white sauce. The lasagne sheets should be completely covered. Sprinkle with Parmesan, cover and cook on Low for 4–6 hours.

I was going to share with you a tripe recipe called callos *but decided this one would appeal to more of you and, sadly, tripe can be hard to find. This is* caldo gallego, *another favourite, from the northern tip of Spain, which I have enjoyed many times in and around La Coruña. Some families serve the broth first then the meats and vegetables, but I prefer it as a stew.*

galician pork and vegetable stew with chorizo

SERVES 4

100 g/4 oz/⅔ cup dried haricot (navy) beans, soaked in boiling water for at least 1 hour or in cold water overnight
450 ml/¾ pt/2 cups chicken or pork stock, made with 1 stock cube
350 g/12 oz belly pork or veal, cut into large chunks
175 g/6 oz piece of raw unsmoked ham, cut into chunks
1 x 110 g/4 oz chorizo, skinned and thickly sliced

1 onion, chopped
1 garlic clove, crushed
1 large turnip, cut into chunks
½ small white cabbage, shredded
450 g/1 lb potatoes, peeled and cut into chunks
Salt and freshly ground black pepper
30 ml/2 tbsp chopped fresh parsley, to garnish

TO SERVE:
Crusty bread and a dish of mixed green and black Spanish olives

1 Drain the beans, tip into a saucepan and cover with cold water. Bring to the boil and boil rapidly for 10 minutes. Tip into the crock pot. Add a little more boiling water, if necessary, so they are just covered. Cover and cook on High for 3 hours.

2 Add all the remaining ingredients, cover and cook on High for 4–5 hours until everything is tender. Taste and re-season, if necessary.

3 Ladle into warm bowls, sprinkle with the parsley and serve with crusty bread and a dish of olives.

The literal translation of this Greek speciality, kleftiko, is 'meat done by thieves'. Traditionally it is put in a clay pot and sealed with a flour and water paste to prevent steam escaping, and sometimes taken to the baker's to be slow-cooked in the bread oven. It can be cooked with just salt, garlic and oregano, but I love the addition of tomatoes, olives and Feta cheese.

slow-roast lamb with olives, tomatoes and feta

SERVES 4

4 lamb shanks
½ lemon
2 garlic cloves, cut into slivers
2 beefsteak tomatoes, skinned and diced
50 g/2 oz/⅓ cup black olives
50 g/2 oz/⅓ cup green olives
8 medium-large potatoes, peeled and halved

Salt and freshly ground black pepper
2.5 ml/½ tsp dried oregano
150 ml/¼ pt/⅔ cup boiling lamb stock, made with ½ stock cube
50 g/2 oz/¼ cup Feta cheese, crumbled
30 ml/2 tbsp chopped fresh parsley

TO SERVE:
Pitta breads and a mixed salad

1 Rub the lamb all over with the lemon. Make several small, deep cuts in the flesh and push a sliver of garlic into each.

2 Put the tomatoes and olives in the base of the crock pot. Put the meat on top and arrange the potatoes around. Season all over with salt and pepper and sprinkle the lamb with the oregano.

3 Pour the stock over, cover and cook on High for 5–6 hours.

4 Transfer the meat and potatoes to warm plates and spoon the tomato and olive mixture over. Sprinkle with the Feta and parsley and serve with pitta breads and a mixed salad.

Variations

The potatoes can be cooked separately, but are much better cooked with the meat to absorb all the rich flavours.

You can use a small whole shoulder or half a leg instead of the lamb shanks if you prefer.

This is from the Basque country and is popular both sides of the border, in France and Spain. I first had it in Anglet, near Biarritz on the French Atlantic coast – I know that's not the Mediterranean, but the recipe earns its place in this chapter because it does have all the right ingredients!

chicken braised in white wine with peppers and tomatoes

SERVES 4

30 ml/2 tbsp olive oil
100 g/4 oz/1 cup lardons (diced bacon)
2 large onions, roughly chopped
2 garlic cloves, crushed
1 green (bell) pepper, diced
30 ml/2 tbsp plain (all-purpose) flour
Salt and freshly ground black pepper
4 chicken portions
1 x 400 g/14 oz/large can of chopped tomatoes

15 ml/1 tbsp tomato purée (paste)
90 ml/6 tbsp dry white wine
5 ml/1 tsp caster (superfine) sugar
1 bouquet garni sachet
A little chopped fresh parsley, to garnish

TO SERVE:
Buttered noodles and a green salad

1   Heat the oil in a frying pan, add the lardons, onions, garlic and diced pepper and fry, stirring, for 2 minutes. Remove from the pan with a draining spoon and reserve.

2   Mix the flour with a little salt and pepper and use to coat the chicken. Fry in the pan until browned on all sides. Transfer to the crock pot and scatter the bacon and onion mixture over.

3   Add any remaining flour to the pan and stir in the tomatoes, tomatoe purée, wine, sugar and a little salt and pepper. Bring to the boil, stirring. Pour over the chicken, tuck in the bouquet garni sachet, cover and cook on High for 3–4 hours.

4   Serve garnished with parsley on a bed of buttered noodles with a green salad.

Cassoulet, *from the Languedoc region of France, is named after the cooking pot in which it is made, the* cassol d'Issel. *There are many different regional variations. One has confit of goose and pigs' trotters, another lamb, bacon and spicy sausage, another fresh and cured pork with coarse pork sausages. My version uses duck, lamb and good, meaty sausages.*

rustic white beans with duck, lamb and sausage

SERVES 4–6

350 g/12 oz/2 cups dried haricot (navy) beans or white kidney beans, soaked in cold water for several hours or overnight
1 litre/1¾ pts/4¼ cups water
1 beef stock cube
2 duck portions, halved
4 traditional coarse-textured pork or venison sausages
4 lamb chops
50 g/2 oz smoked lardons (diced bacon)

1 large onion, chopped
1 large garlic clove, crushed
1 bouquet garni sachet
Salt and freshly ground black pepper
100 g/4 oz/2 cups fresh breadcrumbs
25 g/1 oz/2 tbsp butter
45 ml/3 tbsp chopped fresh parsley

TO SERVE:
A green salad

1 Drain the beans, put in a pan and cover with the water. Bring to the boil and boil rapidly for 10 minutes. Stir in the stock cube.

2 Meanwhile, heat a frying pan. Add the duck and cook, skin-sides down, until the fat runs, then fry on both sides to brown. Lift out of the pan and put in the crock pot. Brown the sausages and chops in the pan and add to the pot.

3 Add the lardons, onion and garlic to the pan and fry for 2 minutes, stirring. Add to the pot.

4 Transfer the beans and their liquor to the crock pot and add the bouquet garni and some salt and pepper. Cover and cook on High for 6–7 hours.

5 When the cassoulet is nearly ready, fry the breadcrumbs in the butter, stirring all the time, until golden. Stir in the parsley.

6 Discard the bouquet garni from the casserole, then press the breadcrumb mixture all over the top. Serve straight from the pot with a green salad.

Choucroute garni is a very filling dish that comes from the Alsace region of France, though it is now served all over the country. You will find market stalls with huge vats of it but it is also served in some classy restaurants! There are Eastern European versions too. Traditionally it uses duck fat for cooking but I find butter works just as well.

sauerkraut with mixed meats and juniper berries

SERVES 4

810 g/scant 2 lb jar of sauerkraut
25 g/1 oz/2 tbsp butter
1 onion, thinly sliced
1 large garlic clove, crushed
6 juniper berries, crushed
2.5 ml/½ tsp ground coriander
   (cilantro)
A good pinch of ground cloves
150 ml/¼ pt/⅔ cup medium-dry
   white wine – ideally a Riesling
   from Alsace
150 ml/¼ pt/⅔ cup pork or chicken
   stock, made with ½ stock cube

Salt and freshly ground black pepper
4 large frankfurters
1 x 450 g/1 lb piece of speck or
   other smoked streaky pork
225 g/8 oz piece of smoked pork
   loin
1 pork hock
1 large bay leaf

TO SERVE:
Plain boiled potatoes and mustard

1   Wash the sauerkraut well, drain thoroughly and place in the crock pot.

2   Heat the butter in a frying pan, add the onion and fry gently, stirring, for 2 minutes to soften. Stir in the garlic, spices, wine, stock and seasoning and bring to the boil. Season well.

3   Meanwhile, put all the meats in the crock pot, pushing them into the sauerkraut. Pour the boiling wine mixture over and tuck in the bay leaf. Cover and cook on High for 5–7 hours.

4   Lift out the pieces of pork and cut into chunks. Spoon the sauerkraut on to plates with a draining spoon and top with the pieces of pork and the frankfurters. Serve hot with potatoes and mustard.

This is a very popular dessert, but delicate custards can be disappointing when cooked in the conventional way. However, using your slow cooker as a bain marie will ensure the custard does not curdle. If you have a kitchen blow torch, you can use it to caramelise the top of the crème brûlée instead of using the grill.

crème brûlée

SERVES 4

2 eggs

75 g/3 oz/⅓ cup caster (superfine) sugar

450 ml/¾ pt/2 cups double (heavy) cream

5 ml/1 tsp natural vanilla essence (extract)

1   Whisk the eggs with 30 ml/2 tbsp of the sugar, the cream and the vanilla. Strain into four ramekin dishes (custard cups).

2   Place in the crock pot with enough boiling water to come half-way up the sides of the dishes. Cover and cook on Low 2–3 hours.

3   Remove the ramekins from the cooker, leave to cool, then chill.

4   Just before serving, sprinkle the tops liberally with the remaining sugar. Place under a preheated grill (broiler) until the sugar has melted and is a rich brown colour.

A TASTE OF
NORTH AMERICA

There is such diversity in the cuisine of North America because of the influence of centuries of immigration from all over the world. It has adapted styles from all other continents, from Native American to New England cuisine, from Creole (originating in Louisianna) to the light, more health-conscious food of California. There are wonderful Canadian specialities, often with a French influence, and Tex Mex – a fusion of Mexican and cowboy fodder and everyone's favourite 'fun' food. You'll also find American Chinese and Pensylvanian Dutch fare... and much more. It is, too, the home of modern fast food but that won't affect us here as we enjoy the pleasures of slow cooking!

This is a typical North American hot dip to serve with salty crackers and raw vegetable sticks. It is one of the most delicious appetisers I know. If you have a large oval crock pot, I suggest you make this in a soufflé (or similar) dish in the pot, with about 2.5 cm/1 in of boiling water around it.

hot shrimp and crab dip

SERVES 6–8

50 g/2 oz/¼ cup unsalted (sweet) butter
350 g/12 oz/1½ cups cream cheese
5 ml/1 tsp paprika
2 spring onions (scallions), finely chopped
2 celery sticks, finely chopped
1 x 170 g/6 oz/small can of white crabmeat, drained

100 g/4 oz cooked, peeled prawns (shrimp), thawed if frozen, drained and chopped
5 ml/1 tsp lemon juice
2.5 ml/½ tsp Worcestershire sauce
A few drops of Tabasco sauce
Salt and freshly ground black pepper

1 Put all the ingredients in the crock pot. Cover and cook on High for about 20 minutes until the butter is melting.

2 Stir well to blend, re-cover and cook for about 30 minutes, stirring occasionally, until piping hot and gently bubbling.

3 Turn down the setting to Low and serve straight from the pot so it keeps hot, or you can serve it as a starter by spooning it into warm ramekins (custard cups) on small plates with crackers and raw veggie sticks surrounding the dishes.

Cod has been fished off Newfoundland and all down the Canadian coast since the late 15th century, with thousands of fishermen flocking to the area from Europe. It was salted to preserve it before its long journey back across the Atlantic. There are numerous versions of this chowder, but this is the best and simplest I know.

newfoundland salt cod chowder

SERVES 6

400 g/14 oz salt cod
40 g/1½ oz/3 tbsp butter
2 celery sticks, chopped
1 onion, chopped
1 large garlic clove, chopped
1 green (bell) pepper, chopped
5 ml/1 tsp paprika
1.5 ml/¼ tsp mixed (apple pie) spice
50 g/2 oz/¼ cup long-grain rice
1 bay leaf
1 x 400 g/14 oz/large can of chopped tomatoes
450 ml/¾ pt/2 cups tomato juice
750 ml/1¼ pts/3 cups chicken stock, made with 1 stock cube
45 ml/3 tbsp tomato ketchup (catsup)
A few drops of Tabasco sauce
5 ml/1 tsp Worcestershire sauce
5 ml/1 tsp caster (superfine) sugar
Freshly ground black pepper
30 ml/2 tbsp chopped fresh parsley, to garnish

1 Soak the cod in cold water for 12 hours or overnight, changing the water twice. Drain.

2 Melt the butter in a saucepan. Add the celery, onion, garlic and chopped pepper and fry, stirring, for 2 minutes. Stir in the paprika and mixed spice, then all the remaining ingredients. Bring to the boil and tip into the crock pot.

3 Add the fish, pushing it well down. Cover and cook on High for 2–3 hours.

4 Lift out the fish and discard the bay leaf. Remove all the fish from the bones and discard the skin. Flake the fish and return it to the soup. Stir, taste and re-season, if necessary. Ladle into warm bowls, garnish with the parsley and serve.

This hearty soup can be made with creamed sweetcorn instead of corn kernels, but you won't need the crème fraîche as well. It was originally made with fresh corn cobs, from which the cook had to scrape off all the kernels with a very sharp knife. Using a can takes away all the hard work!

new england creamy corn chowder

SERVES 4–6

50 g/2 oz unsmoked lardons (diced bacon)
1 large onion, chopped
1 celery stick, chopped
1 large potato, diced
1 x 350 g/12 oz/medium can of sweetcorn
600 ml/1 pt/2½ cups boiling chicken stock, made with 1 stock cube

Salt and white pepper
300 ml/½ pt/1¼ cups milk
30 ml/2 tbsp dried milk powder (non-fat dry milk)
60 ml/4 tbsp crème fraîche (optional)
30 ml/2 tbsp chopped fresh parsley, to garnish

1 Dry-fry the lardons in a frying pan until the fat runs. Add the onion and cook, stirring, for 2 minutes.

2 Tip into the crock pot with the celery, potato and the contents of the can of sweetcorn.

3 Stir in the stock, season, cover and cook on High for 2–3 hours.

4 Blend the milk with the milk powder and stir into the pot. Re-cover and cook for a further 15 minutes.

5 Stir in the crème fraîche, if using, taste and re-season, if necessary. Serve sprinkled with the parsley.

Crawfish are a favourite food in Louisiana and this is a typical Cajun speciality. If you can't get crawfish tails, use king prawns instead. This dish bursts with flavour, and really couldn't be simpler as almost everything is placed in the crock pot at the beginning, with just the crawfish added for the last half hour or so.

crawfish in spicy tomato and sweet pepper sauce

SERVES 4

1 bunch of spring onions (scallions), chopped
4 ripe tomatoes, skinned, seeded and chopped
2 green (bell) peppers, diced
1 garlic clove, crushed
30 ml/2 tbsp plain (all-purpose) flour
200 ml/7 fl oz/scant 1 cup fish stock, made with 1 stock cube
1.5 ml/¼ tsp cayenne pepper
15 ml/1 tbsp tomato purée (paste)
5 ml/1 tsp caster (superfine) sugar

Salt and freshly ground black pepper
2 slices of lemon
350 g/12 oz crawfish tails, thawed if frozen
A few drops of Tabasco sauce (optional)
15 ml/1 tbsp each of snipped fresh chives and chopped fresh parsley and wedges of lime, to garnish

TO SERVE:
Plain boiled rice and a large green salad

1 Put everything except the crawfish tails and Tabasco, if using, in the crock pot. Cook on High for 1 hour.

2 Discard the lemon slices. Add the crawfish, re-cover and cook for a further 15–30 minutes until cooked through and piping hot. Taste and re-season, if necessary, adding a few drops of Tabasco, if liked. Serve on rice, garnished with snipped chives, chopped parsley and lime wedges, with a large green salad.

Chicken wings are often overlooked because they are fiddly to eat, but they are very economical. They cook really well in the slow cooker and the meat will just fall off the bones. You could throw them on the barbie at the end to crisp and brown, if you like, but they are very moreish just moist and tender.

californian barbecued buffalo wings

SERVES 4–6

24 chicken wings
  (about 1 kg/2¼ lb)
1 large garlic clove, crushed
30 ml/2 tbsp clear honey
10 ml/2 tsp made English mustard
120 ml/4 fl oz/½ cup tomato
  ketchup (catsup)

60 ml/4 tbsp tomato purée (paste)
45 ml/3 tbsp red wine vinegar
15 ml/1 tbsp soy sauce
15 ml/1 tbsp Worcestershire sauce
A few drops of Tabasco sauce

1 Cut off the tips of the chicken wings at the first joint and discard.

2 Mix together all the remaining ingredients in a large saucepan, adding Tabasco to taste. Bring to the boil, add the chicken and toss well.

3 Transfer to the slow cooker, cover and cook on High for 2–3 hours until tender and coated in a rich sauce.

SLOW COOKER TIP

The slow cooker is the perfect way to make cranberry sauce to serve with roasted or grilled (broiled) turkey, chicken or even Virginia ham. Follow your usual recipe, but with only half the liquid. Put the ingredients in the crock pot and stir well. Cook on High for about 2 hours or until the fruit 'pops', stirring once. If you have a large crock pot, cook it in a bowl in the centre with enough boiling water to come half-way up the sides.

This traditional New Orleans dish, often known as chicken gumbo, has, of course, many variations. This is one of my favourites. The one thing you can't change, though, is the okra – the quintessential ingredient. For an equally delicious gumbo use king prawns instead of, or half and half with, the chicken. If so, add the prawns for the last 30 minutes of cooking time.

stewed chicken
with peppers, okra and tomato

SERVES 4

15 g/½ oz/1 tbsp butter or margarine
12 button (pearl) onions, peeled but left whole
450 g/1 lb skinless chicken meat, cut into dice
1 rasher (slice) of back bacon, cut into small dice
5 ml/1 tsp ground turmeric
5 ml/1 tsp ground coriander (cilantro)
2.5 ml/½ tsp chilli powder
100 g/4 oz okra (ladies' fingers), trimmed

1 red (bell) pepper, sliced
1 green pepper, sliced
225 g/8 oz/1 small can of chopped tomatoes
15 ml/1 tbsp tomato purée (paste)
1 large bay leaf
2.5 ml/½ tsp dried oregano
300 ml/½ pt/1¼ cups boiling chicken stock, made with 1 stock cube
Freshly ground black pepper
15 ml/1 tbsp chopped fresh parsley

TO SERVE:
Plain boiled rice

1 Melt the butter or margarine in a frying pan. Add the onions and brown for 2 minutes, stirring.

2 Add the chicken, bacon and spices and cook, stirring, for 1 minute. Tip into the crock pot and add the remaining ingredients except the parsley. Cover and cook on High for 3–4 hours.

3 Remove the bay leaf from the gumbo, taste and re-season, if necessary. Spoon the gumbo over rice in warm bowls, sprinkle with the parsley and serve.

This bean dish evolved from New England but is nothing like our everyday canned baked beans in tomato sauce! Try them topped with fried eggs with lots of crusty bread. You should be able to get salt pork from your supermarket or butcher, but if you can't you can use cubes of bacon or even pork sausages instead.

boston baked beans
with rich pork and tomato sauce

SERVES 4

350 g/12 oz/2 cups dried haricot
   (navy) beans, soaked in boiling
   water for at least an hour or in
   cold water overnight
1.2 litres/2 pts/5 cups water
25 g/1 oz/2 tbsp unsalted (sweet)
   butter
1 onion, very finely chopped
225 g/8 oz piece of salt pork,
   rinsed, rinded and diced

A good pinch of ground cloves
5 ml/1 tsp English mustard powder
30 ml/2 tbsp black treacle
   (molasses)
60 ml/4 tbsp tomato purée (paste)
15 ml/1 tbsp balsamic condiment
1 bay leaf
Salt and freshly ground black pepper

1   Drain the beans and place in a large saucepan. Add the water, bring to the boil, part-cover and boil for 15 minutes. Tip into the crock pot.

2   Meanwhile, melt the butter in a frying pan, add the onion and pork and fry quickly for 2–3 minutes to brown. Tip into the pot.

3   Stir in the cloves, mustard, treacle, tomato purée and vinegar. Tuck in the bay leaf and season fairly lightly. Cover and cook on High for 6–8 hours, by which time the beans should be bathed in a rich, dark sauce.

4   Taste and re-season, if necessary, discard the bay leaf and serve.

There will be some ham left over that you could slice for sandwiches after you've enjoyed this fabulous, succulent ham hot. The stock can be strained and used as the basis for a split pea or lentil soup. So you slow cooker will give you a main course and set you off for lunch or supper the next day!

sweet spiced virginia ham with roast peaches

SERVES 6

1.25–1.5 kg/2½–3 lb piece of Virginia (or other sweet-cured) raw ham
1 bay leaf
1 small onion, quartered
12 black peppercorns
30 ml/2 tbsp light brown sugar
30 ml/2 tbsp fresh breadcrumbs

1.5 ml/¼ tsp ground cloves
15 ml/1 tbsp cider vinegar
3 ripe peaches
15 g/½ oz/1 tbsp butter

TO SERVE:
Mustard, mashed potatoes and sweetcorn

1 Put the ham in the crock pot. Add the bay leaf, onion and peppercorns and pour in enough boiling water to just cover the joint. Cover and cook on High for 2–3 hours until tender but not overcooked.

2 Carefully lift the ham out of the crock pot and place in a roasting tin. Remove the rind. Preheat the oven to 190°C/375°F/gas 5/fan oven 170°C.

3 Blend the sugar with the breadcrumbs, cloves and vinegar. Spread over the fat where the rind was removed.

4 Halve the peaches and place around the joint. Dot with the butter and pour 200 ml/7 fl oz/scant 1 cup of the cooking liquid around.

5 Roast in the oven for 30 minutes until the ham is a rich brown and the peaches are tender. Serve the ham in thick slices with the peaches, the roasting juices spooned over, mustard, mashed potatoes and sweetcorn.

There is a story behind this dish. In the nineteenth century, a hunting party went out, leaving one man in camp to prepare a stew for their return, using their provisions of sweetcorn, tomatoes, bacon and butter beans. Annoyed at being left behind and bored, he shot a rabbit, skinned it and threw it in the pot – with this fabulous result!

rabbit and butter bean brunswick stew with sweetcorn and peppers

SERVES 4–6

100 g/4 oz/⅔ cup dried butter (lima) beans, soaked in boiling water for at least an hour or cold water overnight
1 large onion, sliced
450 g/1 lb tomatoes, quartered
1 large potato, diced
1 green (bell) pepper, diced
1 x 200 g/7 oz/small can of sweetcorn

1 prepared rabbit, cut into pieces
50 g/2 oz unsmoked lardons (diced bacon)
2.5 ml/½ tsp dried mixed herbs
Salt and freshly ground black pepper
450 ml/¾ pt/2 cups boiling chicken stock, made with 1 stock cube

TO SERVE:
Crusty bread

1 Drain the beans, cover with cold water, bring to the boil and boil rapidly for 10 minutes. Turn down the heat and simmer for 45 minutes or until tender.

2 Drain the beans and tip into the crock pot. Add all the remaining ingredients. Cover and cook on High for 2–3 hours.

3 Taste and re-season, if necessary. Serve in large bowls with some crusty bread.

Variations

You could substitute a small skinned chicken for the rabbit.

Use a can of butter beans instead of dried if you prefer, in which case start the recipe from step 2.

This is a Greek-American dish – and you can see the similarity between it and Slow-roast Lamb with Olives, Tomatoes and Feta (page 51). When cooked, the joint is bathed in a dark, sticky barbecue sauce. Try it, too, packed into warm pitta bread pockets with some shredded lettuce and cucumber and the minted yoghurt sauce on page 82.

lamb roasted
in barbecue sauce

SERVES 4–6

½ leg or shoulder of lamb, about 1 kg
Juice of ½ small lemon
1 large garlic clove, cut into thin
   slivers
Salt and freshly ground black pepper
75 ml/5 tbsp cider vinegar
75 ml/5 tbsp water
45 ml/3 tbsp golden (light corn)
   syrup
30 ml/2 tbsp tomato purée (paste)

60 ml/4 tbsp tomato ketchup
   (catsup)
30 ml/2 tbsp Worcestershire sauce
1.5 ml/¼ tsp chilli powder
5 ml/1 tsp onion granules
15 ml/1 tbsp cornflour (cornstarch)
30 ml/2 tbsp chopped fresh parsley,
   to garnish

TO SERVE:
Plain boiled rice and a large salad

1   Rub the lamb all over with the lemon half. Make small slits in the flesh and push a sliver of garlic into each one. Place in the crock pot.

2   Put all the remaining ingredients in a saucepan and bring to the boil, stirring. Spoon over the lamb, cover and cook on High for 3–4 hours.

3   Cut the meat into neat pieces, transfer to warm plates and spoon the juices over. Garnish with parsley and serve with rice and a large salad.

You'll find a different version of this ultra-simple, all-American dish in just about every household. Many are served with a barbecue-type sauce (made with ketchup, mustard, sugar and vinegar) but I prefer this one, topped with tomato sauce and cheese. Vary the flavour by experimenting with different stuffing mixes and use any leftovers in sandwiches.

cheese-topped
florida meatloaf

SERVES 4

350 g/12 oz minced (ground) beef
½ x 85 g/3½ oz/small packet of sage
  and onion stuffing mix
175 ml/6 fl oz/¾ cup passata (sieved
  tomatoes)
Salt and freshly ground black pepper
1 small egg, beaten
A little oil or butter for greasing

50 g/2 oz/½ cup grated Cheddar
  cheese
2.5 ml/½ tsp caster (superfine)
  sugar
2.5 ml/½ tsp dried basil

TO SERVE:
Crusty bread and a mixed salad

1   Mix the beef with the stuffing mix, 60 ml/4 tbsp of the passata and some salt and pepper. Add the beaten egg and mix well to bind.

2   Turn the mixture into a greased 450 g/1 lb loaf tin (pan) and cover with foil. Place in the crock pot and add enough boiling water to come half-way up the sides of the pan. Cook on High for 4–5 hours.

3   Remove the pan from the crock pot, leave to stand for 10 minutes, then turn out on to a flameproof dish. Smother with the cheese and flash under a hot grill (broiler), until melted and bubbling.

4   Meanwhile, heat the remaining passata with a little salt and pepper, the sugar and basil.

5   Serve the loaf sliced with the tomato sauce spooned over, with crusty bread and a mixed salad.

A TASTE OF
CENTRAL AND
SOUTH AMERICA

Traditional dishes of the Caribbean, Mexico and South America are exotic, intriguing and different from anywhere else in the world! In Mexico, particularly, chillies are served with just about everything – including ice cream and strawberries! You would think they would smother all other flavours but they don't. Salt and sugar loom large in the cuisine and the chillies add an exciting extra dimension. The tropical climate means loads of glorious fruits, vegetables and, of course, seafood but you'll also find lots of rustic dishes from the nomadic tribes living in deserts and mountains. Just out of interest, the Mexicans serve their food with flour or corn tortillas as a bread accompaniment to their stews and casseroles. You simply put one on the flat of your hand, roll it up with the other hand and use the roll to mop up juices or push the food on to your fork.

This recipe, locro de papa, *comes from Ecuador. At its most basic it is just potatoes and onions in a mild and milky broth, topped with avocado slices. My version is richer and more flavoursome and is topped with an avocado salsa that you can use as an accompaniment to many other dishes – or just as a dip.*

velvet potato soup
with avocado salsa

SERVES 4

1 bunch of spring onions
15 ml/1 tbsp sunflower oil
1 garlic clove, crushed
6 floury potatoes, cut into small dice
15 ml/1 tbsp plain (all-purpose) flour
60 ml/4 tbsp dried milk powder
  (non-fat dry milk)
1 litre/1¾ pts/4¼ cups boiling
  chicken stock made with 1 stock
  cube
Salt and freshly ground black pepper
60 ml/4 tbsp crème fraîche

FOR THE AVOCADO SALSA:
1 ripe avocado, peeled, stoned
  (pitted) and finely diced
10 ml/2 tsp lime juice
1 green chilli, seeded and finely
  chopped
1 green (bell) pepper, finely chopped
Salt and freshly ground black pepper

TO SERVE:
Chilli sauce (optional)

1 Reserve two spring onions for the salsa and finely choped the remainder.

2 Heat the oil in a pan, add the chopped spring onions and the garlic and cook, stirring, for 1 minute to soften slightly without browning.

3 Tip into the crock pot with the potatoes, flour and milk powder. Stir in the stock and some salt and pepper. Cover and cook on High for 3–4 hours.

4 Meanwhile, to make the salsa, chop the reserved spring onions. Roughly crush the avocado in a bowl with the lime juice and stir in the spring onions, chilli and chopped pepper. Season to taste.

5 Purée the cooked soup in a blender or food processor. Taste and re-season. Tip back into the crock pot, stir in the crème fraîche and reheat for 5 minutes. Serve ladled into bowls, topped with a spoonful of the salsa and chilli sauce, if liked.

This Mexican rice dish, known as sopa de arroz, *is often made with the addition of spicy sausage too. For a more substantial dish, you could try topping it with an omelette or fried eggs, which would be very Mexican. Look for the runny red or yellow hot pepper sauce in bottles, rather than chunky salsa, to serve with this.*

mexican rice
with king prawns and chillies

SERVES 4

30 ml/2 tbsp sunflower oil
1 onion, chopped
1 green (bell) pepper, diced
1 red pepper, diced
2 garlic cloves, crushed
1–2 green chillies, seeded and
   chopped
4 tomatoes, chopped
225 g/8 oz/1 cup long-grain rice
450 ml/¾ pt/2 cups boiling fish or
   chicken stock, made with 1 stock
   cube

Salt and freshly ground black pepper
200 g/7 oz thawed frozen raw
   shelled king prawns (jumbo
   shrimp)
1 avocado
5 ml/1 tsp lemon juice
12 stuffed green olives

TO SERVE:
Hot pepper sauce (optional)

1 Heat the oil in a saucepan, add the onion and diced peppers and fry, stirring, for 2 minutes.

2 Stir in the garlic, chillies, tomatoes, rice, stock and some seasoning. Bring to the boil and tip into the crock pot. Cover and cook on High for 2–3 hours. Add the prawns 15 minutes before serving.

3 Meanwhile, peel, stone (pit) and slice the avocado and toss with the lemon juice to prevent browning.

4 Fluff up the rice mixture with a fork. Spoon into bowls and garnish each with some sliced avocado and stuffed olives. Serve with hot pepper sauce, if liked.

You can find versions of this dish throughout Central and South America. Some say what you might think of as the unlikely addition of coffee to the stew is something the cowboys invented; others say the Cubans created it. This version comes from Brazil and is, to my mind, the best of the bunch!

rich brazilian beef with coffee

SERVES 4

700 g/1½ lb braising steak cut into 4 slabs
60 ml/4 tbsp plain (all-purpose) flour
Salt and freshly ground black pepper
45 ml/3 tbsp sunflower oil
2 large onions, sliced
4 carrots, sliced
100 g/4 oz mushrooms, sliced
450 ml/¾ pt/2 cups beef stock, made with 1 stock cube

150 ml/¼ pt/⅔ cup strong black coffee
1 bouquet garni sachet
30 ml/2 tbsp chopped fresh parsley, to garnish

TO SERVE:
Plain boiled rice and butternut squash

1 Coat the beef in the flour, seasoned with a little salt and pepper.

2 Heat half the oil in a frying pan, add the onions and carrots and brown for 3 minutes. Transfer to the crock pot with a draining spoon. Add the mushrooms to the pot.

3 Heat the remaining oil, add the beef and brown quickly all over. Transfer to the pot.

4 Tip any remaining flour into the pan. Blend in the stock and coffee and bring to the boil, stirring. Pour over the meat and add the bouquet garni and a little more salt and pepper. Cover and cook on High for 5–6 hours.

5 Discard the bouquet garni, taste and re-season, if necessary. Garnish with the parsley and serve with rice and butternut squash.

This Haitian speciality, known as griots con sauce ti-malice, *has a sweet flavour that is complemented beautifully by the hot, sharp lime sauce. The combination is quite unusual but they are in fact the perfect flavours to go with rich pork meat. I haven't tried it but I would guess that duck would taste fantastic with the same treatment.*

braised glazed pork with chilli lime sauce

SERVES 4

30 ml/2 tbsp sunflower oil
700 g/1½ lb lean pork, diced
1 bunch of spring onions (scallions) chopped
Grated zest of 1 orange
Juice of 4 oranges
Grated zest and juice of ½ lime
1.5 ml/¼ tsp dried thyme
15 ml/1 tbsp dark brown sugar
Salt and freshly ground black pepper

FOR THE CHILLI LIME SAUCE:
15 g/½ oz/1 tbsp butter
15 ml/1 tbsp sunflower oil
1 large onion, finely chopped
1 small garlic clove, finely chopped
2 green chillies, seeded and finely chopped
60 ml/4 tbsp fresh lime juice (you will need about 3 limes)
Salt

TO SERVE:
Fried sweet potatoes

1   Heat the oil in a saucepan. Add the pork and fry, turning, until it is richly browned.

2   Add all the remaining ingredients to the pan and bring to the boil. Tip into the crock pot, cover and cook on High for 3–4 hours.

3   Meanwhile, to make the sauce, heat the butter and oil in a small saucepan. Add the onion and fry gently, stirring, for 3–4 minutes until soft but not brown. Stir in the garlic, chillies and half the lime juice. Cover and cook on as low a heat as possible for 5 minutes, stirring occasionally. Stir in the rest of the lime juice and season with salt.

4   Serve the sauce at room temperature with the hot pork and fried sweet potatoes.

The ancient Aztecs created this dish – they used chocolate in many surprising ways. If you suppose that cooking a savoury dish with chocolate is just too weird, you are probably thinking of foil-wrapped slabs of sweet milk chocolate! However, the dark, bitter cocoa adds an amazing richness to this beef casserole.

aztec beef and chocolate stew with almonds

SERVES 4

I onion, roughly chopped
2 garlic cloves, roughly chopped
1 green chilli, seeded and chopped
50 g/2 oz/⅓ cup raisins
30 ml/2 tbsp cocoa (unsweetened chocolate) powder
30 ml/2 tbsp water
30 ml/2 tbsp sunflower oil
700 g/1½ lb stewing beef, cubed
5 ml/1 tsp ground cinnamon
A good pinch of ground cloves
2 carrots, sliced
50 g/2 oz/½ cup ground almonds

2 large open field or cultivated mushrooms, with black gills, peeled and chopped
350 ml/12 fl oz/1½ cups beef stock, made with 1 stock cube
Salt and freshly ground black pepper
A few fresh coriander (cilantro) leaves, to garnish

TO SERVE:
Plain boiled rice and French (green) beans

1   Put the onion, garlic, chilli, raisins, cocoa and water in a blender and run the machine until smooth, stopping and scraping down the sides as necessary.

2   Heat the oil in a pan, add the beef and fry quickly to brown on all sides. Add the cocoa paste, spices and carrots and fry for a further 2 minutes, stirring all the time. Tip into the crock pot.

3   Add the ground almonds, mushrooms and stock to the pan and bring to the boil, stirring. Pour into the pot and season with salt and pepper. Cover and cook on High for 5–6 hours.

4   Stir, taste and re-season, if necessary. Serve garnished with coriander leaves on a bed of rice with some French beans.

You really must try this surprisingly good Jamaican dish that blends beef and tomatoes, oregano and cumin with sweet and fragrant papaya. Some varieties of papaya grow to an enormous size – up to 10 kg (22 lb), though you won't find ones this big in your supermarket! You will need unripe fruit, so choose ones that are not soft.

jamaican beef-stuffed papaya with oregano and cumin

SERVES 4

2 large unripe papayas (pawpaws), halved lengthways and seeded (pitted)
30 ml/2 tbsp sunflower oil
1 onion, finely chopped
1 garlic clove, crushed
350 g/12 oz minced (ground) beef
2.5 ml/½ tsp dried oregano
2.5 ml/½ tsp ground cumin
2 tomatoes, skinned, seeded and chopped

1 red chilli, seeded and chopped
15 ml/1 tbsp tomato purée (paste)
A good pinch of caster (superfine) sugar
Salt and freshly ground black pepper
60 ml/4 tbsp freshly grated Parmesan cheese

TO SERVE:
A large mixed salad and corn bread or flat breads

1 If necessary cut a tiny strip off the base of the papayas so they will sit flat, taking care not to cut through the flesh to leave a hole. Place them in the crock pot.

2 Heat the oil in a saucepan. Add the onion and garlic and fry, stirring, for 2 minutes. Add the beef and fry until the meat is no longer pink and all the grains are separate.

3 Stir in all the remaining ingredients except the Parmesan and cook rapidly, stirring, for 5 minutes.

4 Spoon the mixture into the papaya cavities, then over the flesh. Sprinkle with half the Parmesan.

5 Carefully pour enough boiling water round the edge of the crock pot to a depth of 1 cm/½ in. Cover and cook on High for 4–5 hours until the fruit is tender.

6 Carefully transfer to warm serving plates, sprinkle with the remaining Parmesan and serve with a large mixed salad and some corn bread or flat breads.

Mexicans roar with laughter when they hear of our chilli con carne –
which literally means chilli with meat. To them that would be a huge bowl
of chillies with a little meat sauce! Here is the genuine article, which is
much hotter than our versions. We had a similar chilli in Barbados but
without the green pepper, and with red kidney beans instead of pinto.

traditional mexican
carne con chilli

SERVES 4

15 ml/1 tbsp groundnut (peanut) oil
450 g/1 lb minced (ground) beef
1 large onion, chopped
1 green (bell) pepper, chopped
1 large garlic clove, crushed
1 x 400 g/14 oz/large can of
   chopped tomatoes
½ x 200 g/7 oz/small jar of pickled
   jalapeño peppers, drained and
   chopped

5 ml/1 tsp chilli powder
1 beef stock cube
2 x 400 g/14 oz/large cans of pinto
   beans (not drained)
Salt and freshly ground black pepper

TO SERVE:
Grated cheese, finely chopped onion
   (mixed with some fresh chopped
   chillies, if liked) and corn tortilla
   chips

1   Heat the oil in a saucepan, add the beef and onion and fry, stirring, until the meat is no longer pink and all the grains are separate.

2   Add all the remaining ingredients and bring to the boil. Tip into the crock pot, cover and cook on High for 2–3 hours.

3   Taste and re-season, if necessary. Serve with grated cheese, finely chopped onion and corn tortilla chips.

Veracruz is on the Gulf of Mexico and is famous for its seafood. Here a whole fish is cooked with chillies, caperberries, olives and tomatoes – a dish that is now popular all over Mexico. In Mexico they tend to use red snapper or sea bass but I found it is particularly good with mackerel. I have toned down the chilli but feel free to add more if you wish.

veracruzana-style mackerel with hot caperberry and olive sauce

SERVES 4

4 good-sized mackerel, cleaned and heads removed, if preferred
Juice of 1 lime
5 ml/1 tsp coarse sea salt
Freshly ground black pepper
1 green chilli, seeded and finely chopped
30 ml/2 tbsp olive oil
2 onions, thinly sliced
2 garlic cloves, crushed
1 green (bell) pepper, cut into diamond shapes

700 g/1½ lb ripe tomatoes, quartered
5 ml/1 tsp caster (superfine) sugar
8 slices of pickled jalapeño pepper, from a jar
25 g/1 oz pickled caperberries
50 g/2 oz/⅓ cup stuffed green olives
Wedges of lime, to garnish

TO SERVE:
Plain boiled potatoes and an avocado and cucumber salad

1 Rinse the mackerel and pat dry with kitchen paper (paper towels). Makes several slashes on both sides of the flesh. Rub with the lime juice, sea salt, some pepper and the chilli. Lay the fish in the crock pot.

2 Heat the oil in a frying pan. Add the onions, garlic and green pepper and cook, stirring, for 3 minutes. Add all the remaining ingredients and cook for a further 3 minutes. Spoon over the mackerel, cover and cook on Low for 1½–2 hours or until the fish flakes easily with a fork and the tomatoes are cooked but still hold their shape.

3 Transfer the fish and tomato mixture to warm plates. Garnish with lime wedges and serve with potatoes and an avocado and cucumber salad.

This Cuban speciality, picadillo, *is sometimes served with fried plantains and rice and peas. The Cubans add a little annatto, which is an orangey-yellow natural food colouring used in many Central and South American dishes. If you want the authentic colour, add a pinch of turmeric, but I like it without!*

spiced chopped beef
with olives, raisins and fried eggs

SERVES 4

700 g/1½ lb lean braising steak, cut into large cubes
Salt and freshly ground black pepper
30 ml/2 tbsp sunflower oil, plus extra for frying
1 large onion, finely chopped
1 large garlic clove, finely chopped
2 large green (bell) peppers, finely chopped
1 green chilli, seeded and finely chopped

A good pinch of ground cloves
1 x 400 g/14 oz/large can of chopped tomatoes
5 ml/1 tsp caster (superfine) sugar
50 g/2 oz/⅓ cup stuffed green olives
50 g/2 oz/⅓ cup raisins
10 ml/2 tsp distilled white vinegar
4 eggs
15 ml/1 tbsp chopped fresh coriander (cilantro)

1 Put the beef in the crock pot with a little salt and pepper. Cover with boiling water, cover and cook on High for 4–5 hours until meltingly tender.

2 About an hour before the beef will be ready, heat the oil in a saucepan, add the onion and fry, stirring, for 5 minutes. Add all the remaining ingredients except the eggs and coriander, bring to the boil and boil rapidly for about 5 minutes, stirring occasionally, until thick and pulpy. Season to taste.

3 When the beef is cooked, drain it thoroughly (you can use the liquid as stock for soup, if you like) and chop it up. Stir into the tomato mixture and heat through.

4 Heat about 5 mm/¼ in of oil in a frying pan and fry the eggs to your liking.

5 Spoon the beef mixture into shallow bowls, sprinkle with the coriander and top with the eggs.

Arroz poblano is lovely as a light meal, perhaps topped with fried eggs, or as a side dish with meat, fish or poultry. Avocados are dirt cheap throughout the region (as are mangos and numerous other exotics we pay a lot for), which is why they are used in abundance. This dish is popular everywhere but this version comes from Hermosillo in Northern Mexico.

poblano-style rice
with chillies and cheese

SERVES 4

350 g/12 oz/1½ cups long-grain rice
30 ml/2 tbsp sunflower oil
1 onion, finely chopped
1 garlic clove, crushed
1–3 green chillies (according to taste), seeded and chopped
1 litre/1¾ pts/4¼ cups chicken stock, made with 2 stock cubes

Salt and freshly ground black pepper
100 g/4 oz/1 cup grated Cheddar or hard sheep's cheese

TO SERVE:
A large bowl of sliced avocado, tossed in fresh lime juice

1 Wash the rice, drain and spread out on a clean cloth to dry.

2 Heat the oil in a pan. Add the onion and garlic and fry, stirring, for 2 minutes. Add the rice and cook for 2–3 minutes, stirring, until turning golden.

3 Add the chillies, stock and seasoning, bring to the boil and tip into the crock pot. Cover and cook on High for 2–3 hours.

4 Top with the cheese, re-cover and cook for a further 5 minutes until the cheese melts. Serve with sliced avocado tossed in lime juice.

SLOW COOKER TIP
Bananas in Rum
Just put a knob of butter and a couple of heaped tablespoonfuls of brown sugar in the crock pot with a tablespoonful (or two) of rum and a splash of lemon or lime juice. Heat on High until melted and bubbling, stirring once or twice. Add some not-too-ripe bananas (whole or sliced in halves lengthways), turn over in the sauce and cook for about 15 minutes until softening but still holding their shape. Serve with ice cream.

A TASTE OF
NORTH AFRICA
AND THE
MIDDLE EAST

Morocco in North Africa is the closest Arab country to Europe, bordering the Atlantic Ocean and the Mediterranean Sea. The traditions found here spread right through the Arab world and form links with the West – in culinary terms. Egypt, for instance, was the end of the spice route from what used to be known as the East Indies, and from here the sweet spices such as cinnamon and cloves were marketed throughout Europe. These and others are used extensively in the region's cooking, along with lamb, poultry, dried peas, beans and lentils, glorious dried fruits and the fresh vegetables you would associate with the Mediterranean (aubergines, peppers, courgettes and so on). Staples are wheat, usually in the form of couscous or *burghal* (which we call bulghar – cracked wheat) and many types of flat bread; rice, too, is used extensively. Slow cooking is traditional. The tajin (or tagine), for instance, is a stew, cooked slowly in a special sealed earthenware pot of the same name, traditionally over charcoal but it cooks very well in the crock pot.

In this chapter you will find my favourite slow-cooked recipes from Lebanon, Saudi Arabia, Iraq, Iran, Tunisia and, of course, Morocco.

Known as harira, *this is the national soup of Morocco, traditionally served during the thirty days of Ramadan to break the fast at sundown. Almost every household will be preparing its own version, filling the streets with its sweet, spicy perfume. It must be very welcome indeed at the end of a long, hungry day.*

moroccan three-bean soup with lamb and saffron

SERVES 4–6

25 g/1 oz/3 tbsp chick peas (garbanzos)
25 g/1 oz/3 tbsp dried broad (lima) or butter (fava) beans
25 g/1 oz/3 tbsp brown lentils
175 g/6 oz diced stewing lamb
1 large onion, chopped
A pinch of saffron strands
15 ml/1 tbsp paprika
5 ml/1 tsp ground coriander (cilantro)
5 ml/1 tsp ground cumin
5 ml/1 tsp salt

Freshly ground black pepper
1 x 400 g/14 oz/large can of chopped tomatoes
1 litre/1¾ pts/4¼ cups boiling lamb stock, made with 2 stock cubes
30 ml/2 tbsp plain (all-purpose) flour
30 ml/2 tbsp water
50 g/2 oz vermicelli, broken into short lengths
A handful of fresh chopped coriander and 1 lemon, thinly sliced, to garnish

1 Soak the chick peas, beans and lentils overnight in cold water. Drain, place in a saucepan, cover with cold water, bring to the boil and boil rapidly for 10 minutes. Drain and tip into the crock pot.

2 Add all the remaining ingredients except the flour, water and vermicelli. Cover and cook on High for 4–5 hours.

3 One hour before you are ready to serve, blend together the flour and water and stir into the soup with the broken vermicelli. Cover and cook for a further 1 hour until everything is tender.

4 Taste and re-season, if necessary. Ladle into warm bowls, sprinkle with the coriander and add a slice or two of lemon to each bowl.

These delicate parcels are called dolmades *in Greece, from where they originate, and* warak enab bi-zayt *in the Middle East. Although they are a bit fiddly to make, they are well worth it because the flavour is superb. Serve them as part of a mezze selection or salad plate, as finger food at parties – or just enjoy them as a tasty snack.*

rice-stuffed vine leaves with pine nuts and currants

SERVES 4–6

50 g/2 oz/½ cup pine nuts
50 g/2 oz/⅓ cup currants
100 g/4 oz/½ cup short grain
   (pudding) rice
1 garlic clove, crushed
1 small onion, finely chopped
60 ml/4 tbsp chopped fresh parsley
60 ml/4 tbsp chopped fresh mint
1 x 225 g/8 oz/small can of
   chopped tomatoes

2.5 ml/½ tsp salt
Freshly ground black pepper
2.5 ml/½ tsp ground cinnamon
1 vacuum pack of vine leaves, rinsed
   and dried
75 ml/5 tbsp olive oil
Juice of ½ lemon
600 ml/1 pt/2½ cups boiling
   vegetable stock, made with
   1 stock cube

1 Toast the pine nuts in a dry frying pan until golden, then tip into a bowl. Mix in the currants, uncooked rice, garlic, onion, herbs, tomatoes, salt, lots of pepper and the cinnamon.

2 Put a little of the filling on each vine leaf, fold in the sides and roll up. Pack them tightly into the crock pot (this will take a while).

3 Add the oil and lemon juice, then pour the boiling stock over. Cover and cook on High for 3–4 hours or until the rice is cooked.

4 Transfer the rolls to a serving platter with a draining spoon. Leave until cold, then chill before serving.

This dish from Iran is a bit like a Greek moussaka but without the creamy cheese and egg topping and is called tepsi beytinjohn. *I like it with the minted yoghurt sauce spooned over, but this isn't traditional. The preparation is more time-consuming than most of the recipes in this book – but when you sit down to eat you will consider it time well spent!*

beef and aubergine layer with minted yoghurt

SERVES 4

3 aubergines, sliced
Salt
Olive oil
700 g/1½ lb minced (ground) beef
2 large onions, chopped
2 garlic cloves, crushed
2.5 ml/½ tsp ground cinnamon
Freshly ground black pepper
6 tomatoes, sliced
450 ml/¾ pt/2 cups passata (sieved tomatoes)

Juice of 1 small lemon
10 ml/2 tsp clear honey

FOR THE SAUCE:
300 ml/½ pt/1¼ cups thick plain yoghurt
1 garlic clove, crushed
30 ml/2 tbsp chopped fresh mint
Salt and freshly ground black pepper

1 Sprinkle the aubergine slices with salt in a colander. Leave to stand for 15 minutes, then rinse and pat dry on kitchen paper (paper towels).

2 Heat a little oil in a frying pan (skillet) and fry the aubergine slices in batches until brown on both sides, adding more oil as you go.

3 Heat 30 ml/2 tbsp more oil in the pan, add the beef and onions and fry, stirring, until the meat is browned and all the grains are separate. Stir in the garlic and cinnamon and season well.

4 Put a layer of aubergines in the crock pot, then add the beef mixture, then cover with the rest of the aubergines, then top with the tomato slices.

5 Pour the passata into the frying pan with the lemon juice and honey. Bring to the boil, then pour over the tomatoes. Cover and cook on High for 2–3 hours, then remove the lid and cook for a further 30 minutes to remove excess moisture.

6   Meanwhile, to make the sauce, mix the yoghurt with the garlic, mint and a little salt and pepper.

7   Serve the aubergine casserole on small plates with a little minted yoghurt spooned over.

This is a Cypriot version, called kiuvetsi, *of a dish popular throughout Eastern Europe and the Middle East. It is named after the cooking pot in which it is made. It is traditionally cooked with* kritharaki, *a barley-like macaroni, though pearl barley works well in a slow cooker. You could use leftover cooked meat, but add it for the last hour of cooking.*

barley pilaff with chicken and feta

SERVES 4

30 ml/2 tbsp olive oil
1 onion, chopped
1 garlic clove, crushed
350 g/12 oz chicken or turkey stir-fry meat
2 courgettes (zucchini), cut into chunks
225 g/8 oz/2 cups pearl barley
600 ml/1 pt/2½ cups chicken stock, made with 1 stock cube
150 ml/¼ pt/⅔ cup passata (sieved tomatoes)

A good pinch of ground cloves
5 ml/1 tsp ground cinnamon
Salt and freshly ground black pepper
100 g/4 oz/½ cup Feta cheese, cubed
30 ml/2 tbsp chopped fresh coriander (cilantro), to garnish

TO SERVE:
Flat breads and a mixed salad

1   Heat the oil in a frying pan. Add the onion, garlic and chicken or turkey and fry for 2 minutes, stirring. Add the courgettes, then stir in the barley until glistening. Tip into the crock pot.

2   Add the stock and passata to the pan, bring to the boil, then pour into the crock pot. Stir and add the cloves, cinnamon and a little salt and pepper. Cover and cook on High for 2–3 hours.

3   Stir in the Feta, then cover and leave for 5 minutes. Spoon on to warm plates and sprinkle with the coriander. Serve with flat breads and a mixed salad.

A tagine is an earthenware pot used to cook stews over charcoal. Tagines are shaped like an upside-down funnel and are often very colourful and lavishly decorated. The crock pot makes a good alternative, though, as it keeps moisture locked in during cooking and makes sure the meat is meltingly tender.

lamb tagine with apricots and sweet spices

SERVES 4

700 g/1½ lb diced stewing lamb
12 button (pearl) onions, peeled but
   left whole
2 courgettes (zucchini), diced
2 carrots, diced
1 green (bell) pepper, diced
100 g/4 oz/⅔ cup ready-to-eat dried
   apricots, halved
1 large garlic clove, crushed
1 green chilli, seeded and chopped

1.5 ml/¼ tsp ground cinnamon
1.5 ml/¼ tsp ground ginger
Salt and freshly ground black pepper
450 ml/¾ pts/2 cups boiling lamb
   stock, made with 1 stock cube
225 g/8 oz/1⅓ cups couscous
30 ml/2 tbsp tomato purée (paste)
30 ml/2 tbsp chopped fresh
   coriander (cilantro)
30 ml/2 tbsp chopped fresh parsley

1   Put the lamb and prepared vegetables in the crock pot with the apricots, garlic, chilli, spices and a little salt and pepper. Add the boiling stock, cover and cook on High for 3–4 hours.

2   Shortly before you are ready to eat, put the couscous in a bowl and just cover with boiling water. Leave to stand for 5 minutes, then steam over boiling water for 15 minutes.

3   Stir the tomato purée and half the herbs into the tagine. Taste and re-season, if necessary.

4   Spoon the couscous on to serving plates. Spoon the lamb mixture on top and sprinkle with the remaining herbs before serving.

This Tunisian speciality is very simple to make. Fish is so easy to overcook but using a crock pot ensures it does not dry out and spoil. Harissa is an orangey-red coloured paste – a fiery mix of chillies, garlic, tomato, spices and olive oil. It can be also be used as a condiment as well as a cooking ingredient. You could use other white fish fillet, but I like cod loin.

cod loin with harissa and black olives

SERVES 4

4 thick pieces of cod loin
45 ml/3 tbsp plain (all-purpose) flour
Salt and freshly ground black pepper
45 ml/3 tbsp olive oil
1 onion, chopped
1 red (bell) pepper, chopped
1 large garlic clove, crushed
250 ml/8 fl oz/1 cup passata (sieved tomatoes)
10 ml/2 tsp harissa paste
A good pinch of caster (superfine) sugar

1 bay leaf
100 g/4 oz/⅔ cup stoned (pitted) black olives
15 ml/1 tbsp chopped fresh parsley or coriander (cilantro) and wedges of lime or lemon, to garnish

TO SERVE:
Plain boiled potatoes

1 Wipe the fish. Mix the flour with some salt and pepper and use to coat the fish.

2 Heat 30 ml/2 tbsp of the oil in a frying pan, add the fish and brown quickly on both sides. Remove from the pan and set aside.

3 Heat the remaining oil in the pan. Add the onion, chopped pepper and garlic and cook, stirring, for 2–3 minutes. Tip into the crock pot and lay the fish on top.

4 Add the remaining ingredients to the pan, seasoning lightly with salt and pepper, and bring to the boil. Tip over the fish. Cover and cook on Low for 1½–2 hours until the fish flakes easily with a fork.

5 Transfer to warm plates, sprinkle with parsley or coriander, garnish with wedges of lime or lemon and serve with potatoes.

There are numerous versions of this traditional one-pot meal throughout North Africa and the Middle East. In Morocco it would be cooked in a couscoussier – a stew pot with a steamer over the top to cook the couscous. To use the slow cooker, you will need to cook the couscous grains separately. If you like lots of couscous, cook 450 g/1 lb.

moroccan couscous with chicken, lamb and a selection of vegetables

SERVES 4

2 large carrots
2 large courgettes (zucchini)
30 ml/2 tbsp olive oil
2 large onions, chopped
4 small chicken portions
4 lamb chops
2 turnips, cut into quarters
4 tomatoes, skinned, seeded and
  chopped
100 g/4 oz French (green) beans,
  topped, tailed and halved

½ small white cabbage, cut into
  wedges
5 ml/1 tsp ground ginger
1.5 ml/¼ tsp cayenne
2.5 ml/½ tsp ground cumin
5 ml/1 tsp clear honey
15 ml/1 tbsp tomato purée (paste)
Salt and freshly ground black pepper
300 ml/½ pt/1¼ cups chicken stock,
  made with 1 stock cube
350 g/12 oz/2 cups couscous
Chopped fresh coriander (cilantro),
  to garnish

1 Cut each carrot and courgette in half, then each half into quarters to make eight sticks.

2 Heat the oil in a frying pan. Add the onions and fry, stirring, for 2 minutes. Transfer to the crock pot with a draining spoon. Brown the chicken and lamb in the pan, then add to the pot. Add the carrot and courgette sticks, the turnips, tomatoes, beans and cabbage.

3 Add the ginger, cayenne, cumin, honey, tomato purée and plenty of salt and pepper to the pan. Stir in the stock and bring to the boil.

4 Pour the boiling stock over the meat and vegetables, cover and cook on High for 4–5 hours.

5 Shortly before you are ready to eat, cook the couscous according to the packet directions. Fluff up with a fork.

6 Taste the casserole and re-season, if necessary. Pile the couscous on to warm serving plates and make a well in the centre. Lift out the chicken, lamb and vegetables with a draining spoon and pile in the centre. Garnish with coriander and hand the juices separately.

This popular casserole is good served with bulghar (cracked wheat) as a change from couscous. I like to cook the grains, then mix in a handful each of fresh chopped parsley, coriander and mint, some seasoning and a drizzle of olive oil. Make sure you have the crisp green salad with or after the dish to offset its richness.

chicken tagine
with prunes and honey

SERVES 4

4 chicken portions
1 small lemon, halved
25 g/1 oz/2 tbsp butter
2 onions, thinly sliced
1 green (bell) pepper, thinly sliced
5 ml/1 tsp ground cinnamon
2.5 ml/½ tsp dried oregano
100 g/4 oz/⅔ cup ready-to-eat
   stoned (pitted) prunes, halved
30 ml/2 tbsp thick honey

300 ml/½ pt /1¼ cups boiling
   chicken stock, made with
   ½ stock cube
30 ml/2 tbsp tomato purée (paste)
Salt and freshly ground black pepper
50 g/2 oz/½ cup blanched (slivered)
   almonds
30 ml/2 tbsp sesame seeds, toasted

TO SERVE:
A crisp green salad

1 Trim off all excess fat from the chicken and rub all over with the lemon.

2 Heat the butter in a frying pan, add the chicken and quickly brown all over. Transfer to the crock pot.

3 Add the onions and sliced pepper to the pan and fry for 2 minutes, stirring. Tip into the crock pot. Add all the remaining ingredients except the almonds and sesame seeds. Cover and cook on High for 3–4 hours.

4 Taste and re-season, if necessary. Sprinkle with the almonds and sesame seeds and serve with a green salad.

These two salads – takshouka b'tabbouleh – make a great combination, but they are also good when served separately. Try the roasted peppers with plain grilled meats, chicken or fish. The tabbouleh makes an exciting and unusual starter when spooned into lettuce leaves and wrapped up for eating with the fingers.

roasted spiced peppers with cracked wheat salad

SERVES 4

FOR THE PEPPERS:
3 green (bell) peppers, cut into
   sixths
3 red peppers, cut into sixths
4 tomatoes, roughly chopped
2 garlic cloves, finely chopped
2.5 ml/½ tsp cumin seeds
2.5 ml/½ tsp paprika
1 small red chilli, seeded and
   chopped (optional)
Salt and freshly ground black pepper
90 ml/6 tbsp olive oil

FOR THE TABBOULEH:
225 g/8 oz/2 cups bulghar (cracked
   wheat)
600 ml/1 pt/2½ cups boiling water
4 spring onions (scallions), chopped
1 large garlic clove, crushed
60 ml/4 tbsp chopped fresh parsley
60 ml/4 tbsp chopped fresh mint
60 ml/4 tbsp chopped fresh
   coriander (cilantro)
30 ml/2 tbsp lemon juice
60 ml/4 tbsp olive oil
Salt and freshly ground black pepper
Wedges of lime and a few stalks of
   parsley or coriander, to garnish

1   Lay the pepper pieces in the crock pot. Scatter the tomatoes, garlic, cumin, paprika and chilli, if using, over the top. Season well, then trickle the oil all over.

2   Cover and cook on High for 1–2 hours, quickly stirring half-way through cooking, until just soft but still with some texture.

3   Meanwhile, to make the tabbouleh, put the bulghar in a bowl and add the boiling water. Stir thoroughly and stand for 30 minutes.

4   Stir the bulghar with a fork to fluff it up, then mix in the remaining ingredients, seasoning to taste. Remove the crock pot from the base to allow it to cool quickly (but don't put it directly on a cold surface – use a trivet or cork mat).

5   When ready to serve, spoon the tabbouleh on to plates and top with the pepper salad. Garnish with lime wedges and stalks of parsley or coriander and serve warm or cold.

This lively mixture of spiced vegetables, shakshsuka, *is perfect cooked in the slow cooker. Because the vegetables don't take that long to cook, I have used canned chick peas in this instance. You could use dried and soak and cook them before adding to the stew. This makes a really satisfying vegetarian dish.*

tunisian ratatouille
with chick peas and eggs

SERVES 4

30 ml/2 tbsp olive oil
1 onion, sliced
5 ml/1 tsp ground turmeric
5 ml/1 tsp ground cumin
2.5 ml/½ tsp dried chilli flakes
1 aubergine, sliced
1 red (bell) pepper, sliced
1 green pepper, sliced
2 courgettes (zucchini), sliced
1 garlic clove, crushed
2 beefsteak tomatoes, skinned and
  chopped
1 x 425 g/15 oz/large can of chick
  peas (garbanzos), drained
Salt and freshly ground black pepper

15 ml/1 tbsp tomato purée (paste)
150 ml/¼ pt/⅔ cup vegetable stock,
  made with 1 stock cube
30 ml/2 tbsp mango chutney
50 g/2 oz/⅓ cup sultanas (golden
  raisins)
5 ml/1 tsp clear honey
4 eggs
15 ml/1 tbsp chopped fresh parsley
15 ml/1 tbsp chopped fresh
  coriander (cilantro)
30 ml/2 tbsp toasted sesame seeds,
  to garnish

TO SERVE:
Flat breads

1   Heat the oil in a large saucepan, add the onion and fry, stirring, for 2 minutes. Add the spices and fry for a further 30 seconds.

2   Add the aubergine, sliced peppers, courgettes, garlic and tomatoes and stir to coat in the spices and oil. Tip into the crock pot. Add the chick peas and some salt and pepper.

3   Blend the tomato purée with the stock, chutney, sultanas and honey in the saucepan. Bring to the boil and add to the pot. Cover and cook on High for 2–3 hours, stirring once, until the vegetables are cooked but still have some 'bite'.

4   Taste and re-season, if necessary. Make four wells in the mixture and break an egg into each. Cover and cook for a further 10–15 minutes or until the eggs are cooked to your liking. Carefully spoon on to plates, sprinkle with the herbs and sesame seeds and serve with flat breads.

This dish is often known just as 'flan' and is popular all over the Middle East and Europe – in fact it's probably served all over the world! It is so easy to make in the slow cooker, and you will get perfect results every time. I've made one big one, but you could make individual creams, in which case the cooking time will be halved.

caramel cream

SERVES 6

175 g/6 oz/¾ cup caster (superfine) sugar
600 ml/1 pt/2½ cup milk

4 eggs
1.5 ml/¼ tsp vanilla essence (extract)

1　Put 100 g/4 oz/½ cup of the sugar in a small heavy-based pan. Heat it gently until it dissolves, then boil rapidly for a few minutes until it turns a deep golden-brown.

2　Immediately pour the caramel into the base of a 1 litre/1¾ pt/ 4¼ cup soufflé dish or pudding basin. Quickly swirl the dish so the caramel almost coats the base before it starts to set.

3　Whisk the milk, eggs and remaining sugar with the vanilla essence. Strain into the soufflé dish, cover with foil and stand the dish in the crock pot. Add enough boiling water to come half-way up the sides of the dish. Cover and cook on Low for 5–6 hours until just set.

4　Leave to cool, then chill. Loosen the edge before turning out into a serving dish.

A TASTE OF
CENTRAL AND SOUTHERN AFRICA

Food and music are integral parts of African social life. As in many countries, every household will offer guests little snacks and a drink even if they arrive unexpectedly. Kindness and friendliness are something you will find everywhere – even in the poorest areas.

Many foods are traditional, handed down through the generations, with regional differences. There are influences from all over Asia, as well as Europe, particularly in Southern Africa thanks to the Dutch settlers. Beans, lentils and vegetables are the main foods, with meat used as a flavouring rather than a main ingredient in many cases. The staples tend to be yams, plantains, cassava and sweet and ordinary potatoes. Coconuts are used widely and chilli and ginger are popular spices. Palm oil is used extensively but it is quite distinctive, with a bright orange colour. There is no real substitute but I have found that using peanut oil and a little sweet paprika gives the right colour, if a milder flavour. Tropical fruits abound – guavas, mangos, papayas, pineapples and avocados are seen everywhere.

This is a staple throughout Africa, with, as usual, many variations.
Traditionally it uses a groundnut paste; the nearest equivalent we have to
it is peanut butter, which I find works well. In African households, you
may have all yam in the soup but I find it nicer adding some sweet
potato too.

spicy peanut soup
with yam and sweet potato

SERVES 4

15 ml/1 tbsp peanut (groundnut) oil
1 onion, chopped
30 ml/2 tbsp tomato purée (paste)
75 ml/5 tbsp smooth peanut butter
1.5 ml/¼ tsp chilli powder
2.5 ml/½ tsp ground cumin
5 ml/1 tsp grated fresh root ginger
1.2 litres/2 pts/5 cups chicken or
  vegetable stock, made with
  2 stock cubes

1 small yam, peeled and cut into
  small dice
1 sweet potato, peeled and cut into
  small dice
5 okra (ladies' fingers), trimmed and
  sliced
Salt and freshly ground black pepper
15 ml/1 tbsp chopped fresh
  coriander (cilantro)

1 Heat the oil in a frying pan, add the onion and fry gently for
2 minutes.

2 Blend in the tomato purée, peanut butter, spices and stock. Bring
to the boil, stirring.

3 Put the yam, sweet potato and okra in the crock pot. Pour the
peanut butter mixture over and season lightly. Cover and cook on
High for 3–4 hours until all the vegetables are tender.

4 Stir, taste and re-season, if necessary. Serve sprinkled with the
coriander to garnish.

As I said in the introduction to this chapter, many soups in Africa are main meals. This is a hearty stew-like soup, which sometimes has black-eyed beans instead of the lentils but I like the thickened consistency the cooked lentils give to the dish. Use a butternut squash instead of pumpkin and a plantain instead of the banana, if you prefer.

west african lamb and pumpkin soup

SERVES 4

1 onion, roughly chopped
225 g/8 oz pumpkin flesh, diced
2 turnips, diced
2 carrots, diced
450 g/1 lb diced stewing lamb
1 piece of cinnamon stick
5 ml/1 tsp ground turmeric
2.5 ml/½ tsp caraway seeds
1 green chilli, seeded and chopped

1 bay leaf
175 g/6 oz/1 cup red lentils
1 litre/1¾ pts/4¼ cups lamb stock, made with 1 stock cube
Salt and freshly ground black pepper
1 large under-ripe banana
15 ml/1 tbsp chopped fresh coriander (cilantro)

1 Put the onion, pumpkin, turnips and carrots in the crock pot and place the lamb on top. Add the cinnamon stick and sprinkle with the turmeric, caraway and chilli. Tuck in the bay leaf.

2 Put the lentils in a saucepan with the stock and bring to the boil. Pour over the lamb and season well. Cover and cook on High for 3–4 hours.

3 When you are nearly ready to eat, cut the banana into diagonal slices and add to the pot. Cover and cook for 15 minutes more.

4 Taste and re-season, if necessary. Discard the cinnamon stick and bay leaf and serve sprinkled with the coriander.

Zigni is standard fare in Ethiopia, though the meat used can vary and different vegetables and flavourings might be used. However, this is my favourite version as the ingredients are all readily available and, even though it is simplicity itself to prepare, the finished dish is full of wonderful flavours.

ethiopian braised sweet-spiced beef with tomatoes

SERVES 4

450 g/1 lb thin-cut beef frying steak
25 g/1 oz/2 tbsp butter
2 large onions, finely chopped
1 garlic clove, crushed
2 beefsteak tomatoes, chopped
15 ml/1 tbsp tomato purée (paste)
1 red (bell) pepper, chopped
150 ml/¼ pt/⅔ cup water

Salt and freshly ground black pepper
1.5 ml/¼ tsp ground cloves
2.5 ml/½ tsp ground cumin
2.5 ml/½ tsp dried oregano
30 ml/2 tbsp chopped fresh parsley

TO SERVE:
Plain boiled rice

1 Lay the meat in the crock pot.

2 Melt the butter in a pan, add the onions and garlic and fry for 2 minutes, stirring.

3 Add all the remaining ingredients except the parsley. Bring to the boil and pour over the beef. Cover and cook on High for 4–6 hours (depending on the quality of the beef).

4 Taste and re-season, if necessary. Sprinkle with the parsley and serve with rice.

My mother-in-law brought this recipe back with her from Cape Town in the early 1980s. The meat cooks to melting tenderness in the slow cooker and is then finished off in the oven until the potato topping is enticingly golden-brown. The water chestnuts add an interesting – and highly pleasurable – crunchy texture.

potato-topped cape beef pot with water chestnuts

SERVES 4

45 ml/3 tbsp cornflour (cornstarch)
Salt and freshly ground black pepper
700 g/1½ lb braising steak, diced
1 large onion, chopped
100 g/4 oz button mushrooms, sliced
450 ml/¾ pt/2 cups boiling beef stock, made with 1 stock cube

1 bay leaf
3 large potatoes, sliced
227 g/8 oz/1 small can of water chestnuts, drained and sliced
298 g/10½ oz/1 medium can of condensed mushroom soup

TO SERVE:
Minted peas, tossed in a little butter

1 Mix the cornflour with a little salt and pepper and use to coat the meat. Put the onion in the crock pot with the meat and mushrooms. Add the boiling stock, bay leaf and a little salt and pepper. Stir, cover and cook on High for 5–6 hours.

2 When the meat is nearly ready, slice the potatoes and boil in lightly salted water for 3 minutes. Drain.

3 Discard the bay leaf from the meat, then tip the contents of the crock pot into an ovenproof serving dish. Add the water chestnuts. Spoon half the soup over and spread out gently.

4 Arrange the potatoes in overlapping slices on top. Mix the remaining soup with 45 ml/3 tbsp water to make it a just pourable consistency. Spread over the surface of the potatoes.

5 Bake in a preheated oven at 200°C/400°F/gas 6/fan oven 180°C for about 50 minutes or until golden-brown on top and piping hot. Serve with minted peas tossed in a little butter.

Jan Van Riebeeck arrived in South Africa with new settlers in 1652 to establish a revictualling station on behalf of a Dutch maritime trading company. Big game was plentiful in the country – but the settlers were not skilled hunters. What meat they used was usually mutton bartered from the Hottentots. Cooked this way, it takes on a rich, gamey flavour.

van riebeeck's
mock venison stew

SERVES 4

2 onions, roughly chopped
1 garlic clove, crushed
700 g/1½ lb diced stewing mutton or
    lamb
100 g/4 oz piece of speck, diced
½ small lemon
2 cloves
2.5 ml/½ tsp ground coriander
    (cilantro)
2.5 ml/½ tsp ground ginger

Salt and freshly ground black pepper
45 ml/3 tbsp cornflour (cornstarch)
200 ml/7 fl oz/scant 1 cup red wine
200 ml/7 fl oz/scant 1 cup beef
    stock, made with 1 stock cube
5 ml/1 tsp caster (superfine) sugar

TO SERVE:
Plain boiled rice and quince or
    redcurrant jelly (clear conserve)

1   Spread out the onion and garlic in the crock pot. Add the mutton or lamb and the speck.

2   Stud the lemon with the cloves and put in the pot with the other spices, seasoning well with salt and pepper.

3   Blend the cornflour with the wine, stock and sugar in a saucepan and bring to the boil, stirring, until thickened. Pour over the meat, cover and cook on High for 5–6 hours.

4   Stir well, taste and re-season, if necessary. Serve with rice and quince or redcurrant jelly.

This South African dish is usually made in the oven so it has a brown surface. I find, however, that the dish cooks perfectly in the slow cooker without drying out, and sprinkling it with toasted coconut makes it even better! If you have a large pot, put the bobotie in a round 1.5 litre/2¹/₂ pt/ 6 cup dish with enough boiling water to come half-way up the sides.

curried beef and almond bake with eggs

SERVES 4

1 thick slice of wholemeal bread
250 ml/8 fl oz/1 cup milk
30 ml/2 tbsp sunflower oil
1 onion, chopped
450 g/1 lb minced (ground) beef or lamb
30 ml/2 tbsp mild curry powder
15 ml/1 tbsp lemon juice
15 ml/1 tbsp apricot jam (conserve)
8 ready-to-eat dried apricots, chopped

50 g/2 oz/⅓ cup raisins
50 g/2 oz/½ cup flaked (slivered) almonds
2.5 ml/½ tsp dried basil
Salt and freshly ground black pepper
2 eggs, beaten
60 ml/4 tbsp desiccated (shredded) coconut

TO SERVE:
Plain boiled rice and mango or another sweet chutney

1 Soak the bread in the milk.

2 Heat the oil in a saucepan. Add the onion and meat and fry, stirring, until the meat is no longer pink and all the grains are separate. Stir in the curry powder and cook for a further 1 minute, stirring. Remove from the heat.

3 Beat the soaked bread and the milk into the meat with all the remaining ingredients except the coconut.

4 Tip into the crock pot, cover and cook on High for 3–4 hours until set.

5 Meanwhile, toast the coconut in a frying pan until golden. Tip out of the pan immediately to prevent it burning.

6 Sprinkle the top of the bobotie with the toasted coconut and serve with rice and chutney.

As I said in the chapter introduction, stews from this part of the world normally have just a little meat to add flavour – cattle and sheep are a sign of wealth so are rarely eaten. I have used rather more pork than a local cook would, but I think you'll find the flavour very good indeed. East Africans would eat this with ugali, a dough made from maize.

east african pork and broad bean stew with garlic and coriander

SERVES 4

30 ml/2 tbsp groundnut (peanut) oil
1 large onion, chopped
5 ml/1 tsp ground cinnamon
450 g/1 lb diced pork
450 g/1 lb shelled broad (fava) beans, thawed if frozen
150 ml/¼ pt/⅔ cup passata (sieved tomatoes)
150 ml/¼ pt/⅔ cup chicken or pork stock, made with ½ stock cube

5 ml/1 tsp caster (superfine) sugar
2.5 ml/½ tsp salt
Freshly ground black pepper
3 garlic cloves, crushed
45 ml/3 tbsp chopped fresh coriander (cilantro)

TO SERVE:
Polenta or mashed potatoes

1   Heat half the oil in a saucepan, add the onion and fry, stirring, for 2 minutes. Stir in the cinnamon and pork and fry for a further 2 minutes. Tip into the crock pot. Add the beans.

2   Put the passata and stock in the pan with the sugar, salt and some pepper. Bring to the boil and pour into the pot. Stir, cover and cook on High for 4–5 hours until the meat is tender.

3   When the stew is nearly ready, heat the remaining oil in a frying pan, add the garlic and coriander and fry for 1 minute, stirring. At the end of cooking, stir this into the stew and leave for 5 minutes to allow the flavour to seep in.

4   Serve with polenta or mashed potatoes.

This South African dish makes a lovely light lunch or supper. You could put some cooked, peeled prawns or some sliced button mushrooms in the base of the squash before adding the custard. If so, you may need to use a small egg and reduce the cheese by 25 g/1 oz/2 tbsp so the mixture will still fit into the squash cavities.

cape acorn squash with chilli herb custard

SERVES 4

2 acorn squash
100 g/4 oz/½ cup white soft cheese
1 garlic clove, crushed
1 small green chilli, seeded and
    chopped
15 ml/1 tbsp chopped fresh parsley
15 ml/1 tbsp chopped fresh
    coriander (cilantro)

15 ml/1 tbsp snipped fresh chives
1 large egg
30 ml/2 tbsp milk
Salt and freshly ground black pepper
A few chive stalks, to garnish

TO SERVE:
Crusty bread and a tomato and
    avocado salad

1 Halve the squashes and scoop out the seeds. Place in the crock pot and pour in about 2.5 cm/1 in boiling water to surround them. Cover and cook on High for 2 hours until just tender.

2 Beat together the remaining ingredients, seasoning to taste. Spoon into the cavities in the squashes. Cover and cook on Low for 2–3 hours until the custard has set.

3 Transfer to plates, garnish with a few chive stalks and serve with crusty bread and a tomato and avocado salad.

This is popular throughout Western Africa, particularly in Sierra Leone. You should be able to find palm oil in large supermarkets or specialist food shops, but if you don't want to buy it specially you could substitute groundnut oil and, if liked, add 5 ml/1 tsp of sweet paprika to give a more authentic colour.

green pepper chicken
with spinach and peanut sauce

SERVES 4

30 ml/2 tbsp palm oil
2 onions, chopped
1 garlic clove, crushed
2 beefsteak tomatoes, skinned and
   chopped
1 green chilli, seeded and chopped
1 green (bell) pepper, diced
100 g/4 oz/1 cup raw peanuts
60 ml/4 tbsp peanut butter

350 ml/12 fl oz/1½ cups chicken
   stock, made with 1 stock cube
225 g/8 oz thawed frozen leaf
   spinach, squeezed thoroughly
Salt and freshly ground black pepper
4 chicken breasts

TO SERVE:
Plain boiled rice

1 Heat the oil in a saucepan, add the onions and garlic and fry for 2 minutes, stirring. Stir in all the remaining ingredients except the chicken breasts and bring to the boil.

2 Put the chicken breasts in the crock pot and pour the sauce over. Cover and cook on High for 3–4 hours.

3 Taste and re-season, if necessary. Serve with rice.

SLOW COOKER TIP
You can use your slow cooker to cook couscous or bulghar (cracked wheat). Simply put the grains in the pot with boiling water or stock as usual. Stir, cover and cook on Low for 30 minutes or until you are ready to serve. Fluff up with a fork before serving.

This is a Kenyan dish, with Indian influences, known as kuku, which usually has more lemon juice than I have added. I don't like it too sharp but by all means add more if you like it! As with so many recipes, there are versions from neighbouring countries too – in fact from throughout the Swahili-speaking region.

coriander chicken with mung beans and coconut

SERVES 4

5 ml/1 tsp ground ginger
2.5 ml/½ tsp ground coriander (cilantro)
1 garlic clove, crushed
4 chicken portions
100 g/4 oz/⅔ cup mung beans, soaked in boiling water for at least 1 hour or in cold water overnight
30 ml/2 tbsp corn or sunflower oil
1 onion, chopped

1 green chilli, seeded and chopped
2 tomatoes, chopped
1 x 400 g/14 oz/large can of coconut milk
15 ml/1 tbsp lemon juice
Salt and freshly ground black pepper
15 ml/1 tbsp chopped fresh coriander

TO SERVE:
Chapattis and a green salad

1   Mix the ginger with the coriander and garlic. Rub all over the chicken and leave to marinate.

2   Meanwhile, drain the beans. Place them in a saucepan, add boiling water and boil for 30–40 minutes or until soft. Drain and mash with a potato masher.

3   Heat the oil in a large frying pan, add the onion and chilli and fry for 2 minutes, stirring. Transfer to the crock pot with a draining spoon. Add the tomatoes to the pot.

4   Add the chicken to the frying pan and brown quickly on all sides. Transfer to the pot.

5   Tip the coconut milk and lemon juice into the saucepan, add the mashed mung beans and some salt and pepper and bring to the boil. Pour over the chicken. Cover and cook on High for 3–4 hours.

6   Add the coriander, taste and re-season, if necessary. Serve with chapattis and a green salad.

This is a wonderful blend of magical flavours. Cooking the fruits slightly with a little sugar and lime juice helps mingle the flavours and makes them lovely and juicy. Try it with other tropical fruits too, but make sure you use fairly thick pieces so they don't overcook. Served with chilled, extra thick coconut milk this dish is an amazing experience!

east african
warm fruit salad

SERVES 4–8

1 small fresh pineapple
2 mangos
2 bananas
2 oranges
45 ml/3 tbsp light brown sugar
Juice of 2 limes

1 passion fruit
1 x 400 g/14 oz/large can of extra-
    thick coconut milk, chilled

TO SERVE:
Crisp thin biscuits (cookies)

1   Cut off the top and base off the pineapple, then cut the fruit into eight slices. Slice the skin away from each piece. Cut the skin off the mangos, then cut the fruit into thick strips following the line of the stone (pit). Cut the bananas into thick diagonal slices. Cut all the skin and pith off the oranges, then cut into round slices. Lay all the fruits in the crock pot.

2   Mix together the sugar and lime juice and spoon over the fruits. Halve the passion fruit and scoop the seeds and juice into the pot.

3   Cover and cook on High for 30–60 minutes until the juices are running from the fruits.

4   Spoon on to plates, top with a spoonful of chilled extra-thick coconut milk and serve with crisp thin biscuits.

A TASTE OF
SOUTHERN ASIA

I have included India, Pakistan and Bangladesh in this section. Curries are an integral part of the cuisine from the whole area. Rice is the staple, but with the addition of both leavened and unleavened breads. Many of the foods are cooked in ghee (clarified butter) but vegetable, coconut and mustard oil are also used, usually in a clay pot, wok or steamer. The food is rich and colourful, steeped in spices (but not always fiery) and herbs. Ginger, garlic and chillies are used extensively but also coconut cream and milk and a wealth of vegetables, lentils and other pulses.

Indian food is largely vegetarian, with main meals consisting of lentil and vegetable dishes, with yoghurt, pickles, chutneys and chapattis or rice. But fish, meat and chicken are eaten as well, the meat often being marinated to tenderise it before cooking. Pakistan is famous for its street food. Apparently, many people buy it to take home for feasts and celebrations – a far cry from UK burger vans!

The tandoor is a clay oven. For tandoori chicken you would need the fire of a hot oven to get that scorched look to the meat. But tandoori fish is a much softer, more delicate creation and the crock pot cooks it beautifully. I have to admit I have never had this in India – I created this recipe back in the 1970s but it was too good to leave out of this book!

tandoori fish
with avocado sambal

SERVES 4

4 pieces of thick white fish fillet, about 150 g/5 oz each
150 ml/¼ pt/⅔ cup thick plain yoghurt
15 ml/1 tbsp lemon juice
5 ml/1 tsp ground cumin
5 ml/1 tsp ground coriander (cilantro)
2.5 ml/½ tsp ground turmeric
5 ml/1 tsp paprika
2.5 ml/½ tsp chilli powder
A good pinch of salt

FOR THE SAMBAL:
1 avocado, peeled, stoned (pitted) and finely diced
1 small onion, finely chopped
1 green chilli, seeded and chopped
25 g/1 oz/3 tbsp sultanas (golden raisins)
Juice of ½ lime or lemon
15 ml/1 tbsp chopped fresh coriander
Salt and freshly ground black pepper
A few torn fresh coriander leaves and wedges of lime or lemon, to garnish

TO SERVE:
Pilau rice

1   Lay the fish in a shallow dish that will take it in one layer. Mix together the yoghurt, lemon juice, spices and salt and spoon over the fish. Turn the fish over in the mixture to coat completely, then leave to marinate for 2 hours, turning and basting occasionally.

2   Transfer the fish to the crock pot, leaving behind any excess marinade. Cover and cook on Low for 1 hour.

3   Meanwhile, to make the sambal, mix together all the ingredients and season to taste. Spoon into a small dish and chill until ready to serve.

4   Transfer the fish to warm plates. Garnish with a few torn coriander leaves and wedges of lime or lemon and serve with the sambal and pilau rice.

Maybe this murgh tikka masala *should be in the North European section, not the Southern Asian, but it doesn't really matter whether it originated in Northern India or Northern England because it is a great dish and very popular. It is important to use thick Greek-style yoghurt, not a very low-fat one, and double cream to give the sauce a luscious, rich creaminess.*

mild chicken curry
with ginger cream and almonds

SERVES 4

1 small sprig of mint
1 onion, quartered
1 large garlic clove, halved
1 cm/½ in piece of fresh root
   ginger, peeled and roughly
   chopped
1 green chilli, seeded and roughly
   chopped
Juice of 1 lime
15 ml/1 tbsp sunflower oil
30 ml/2 tbsp tomato purée (paste)
10 ml/2 tsp paprika
2.5 ml/½ tsp ground coriander
   (cilantro)

2.5 ml/½ tsp ground cumin
2.5 ml/½ tsp ground turmeric
5 ml/1 tsp garam masala
5 ml/1 tsp salt
200 ml/7 fl oz/scant 1 cup plain
   Greek-style yoghurt
700 g/1½ lb skinless chicken breast,
   cut into bite-sized pieces
30 ml/2 tbsp ground almonds
30 ml/2 tbsp double (heavy) cream
Wedges of lime, to garnish

TO SERVE:
Pilau rice or naan bread

1   Strip the mint leaves off the central stalk. With the motor of a food processor running, drop in the mint leaves, onion, garlic, ginger, chilli, lime juice and half the oil, stopping to scrape down the sides as necessary, until you have a coarse paste.

2   Add the tomato purée, ground spices and salt. Run the machine until well blended.

3   Heat the remaining oil in a frying pan, add the paste and fry for 1 minute. Stir in the yoghurt and bring to the boil.

4   Put the chicken in the crock pot and pour the sauce over. Stir well. Cover and cook on High for 3–4 hours

5   Stir in the ground almonds and cream. Taste and re-season, if necessary. Garnish with wedges of lime and serve with pilau rice or naan bread.

Bhuna just means sautéed meat – the chicken is fried first before stewing in the spicy sauce to create this murgh bhuna masala. It should be just coated in sauce, not swimming in it! However, cooking in a crock pot is a moist method and so the result is not as dry as when this dish is cooked conventionally (but I think it's all the better for that).

spiced chicken with tomatoes

SERVES 4

15 ml/1 tbsp sunflower oil
25 g/1 oz/2 tbsp ghee or butter
4 skinless chicken breasts
2 green chillies, seeded and chopped
2 large onions, finely chopped
1 large garlic clove, crushed
10 ml/2 tsp ground cardamom
1.5 ml/¼ tsp ground cloves
5 ml/1 tsp ground ginger
2.5 ml/½ tsp ground turmeric

225 g/8 oz/1 small can of chopped tomatoes
Salt and freshly ground black pepper
30 ml/2 tbsp chopped fresh coriander (cilantro)

TO SERVE:
Naan bread, cucumber raita (yoghurt flavoured with chopped mint and cucumber) and mango chutney

1 Heat the oil and ghee or butter in a frying pan. Add the chicken and brown quickly all over. Transfer to the crock pot.

2 Add the chillies, onions and garlic to the pan and fry for 2 minutes, stirring.

3 Add all the remaining ingredients except the coriander to the pan and bring to the boil. Tip into the crock pot. Cover and cook on High for 2–3 hours.

4 Taste and re-season, if necessary. Lift the chicken out of the sauce. Tip the sauce into a saucepan, bring to the boil and boil rapidly until well reduced. Return the chicken to the sauce.

5 Spoon on to warm plates and sprinkle with the coriander. Serve with naan bread, cucumber raita and mango chutney.

Palak gosht *is a popular dish from the Punjab in Northern India. Because it uses lamb neck fillets, which the slow cooker will make wonderfully tender, it doesn't take as long to cook as some other curries. As a variation, you could try using diced chicken breast instead of the lamb to make* palak murgh.

mild spiced lamb
with spinach and raisins

SERVES 4

15 ml/1 tbsp sunflower oil
1 large onion, chopped
1 garlic clove, crushed
700 g/1½ lb lamb neck fillet, cut into thick slices
5 ml/1 tsp grated fresh root ginger
30 ml/2 tbsp mild curry powder
5 ml/1 tsp paprika

1 small piece of cinnamon stick
5 ml/1 tsp salt
450 g/1 lb fresh spinach
25 g/1 oz/3 tbsp raisins

TO SERVE:
Pilau rice, mango chutney and lime pickle

1   Heat the oil in a saucepan. Add the onion and garlic and fry, stirring, for 2 minutes.

2   Add the lamb and all the spices and the salt and cook, stirring, until the meat is browned on all sides. Tip into the crock pot.

3   Wash the spinach thoroughly and shake off the excess moisture. Roughly chop and add to the crock pot with the raisins. Cover and cook on High for 2–3 hours.

4   Discard the cinnamon stick, taste and re-season, if necessary. Serve with pilau rice, mango chutney and lime pickle.

This keema curry is eaten in most Indian households and the recipe here was given to me by a London spice merchant. The cream is not used in some versions, but adding it does make the whole dish much richer tasting. It doesn't have an endless list of ingredients and is so quick and easy to prepare that it will soon become a family favourite.

minced beef curry with ginger

SERVES 4

30 ml/2 tbsp sunflower oil
2 onions, chopped
2 garlic cloves, crushed
10 ml/2 tsp grated fresh root ginger
450 g/1 lb minced (ground) beef
30 ml/2 tbsp curry powder
200 ml/7 fl oz/scant 1 cup water

30 ml/2 tbsp tomato purée (paste)
Salt
60 ml/4 tbsp double (heavy) cream
    (optional)

TO SERVE:
Plain boiled rice and mango chutney

1   Heat the oil in a saucepan. Add the onions, garlic, ginger and beef and cook, stirring, until the meat is no longer pink and all the grains are separate.

2   Stir in the curry powder and cook for 2 minutes.

3   Stir in the water and tomato purée and add salt to taste. Bring to the boil, then tip into the crock pot. Cover and cook on High for 2–3 hours.

4   Stir in the cream, if using, taste and re-season, if necessary. Serve with rice and mango chutney.

There are loads of different versions of gosht biryani, but this one lends itself to slow-cooking better than most. The cubes of lamb are sautéed with the onions and spices, then the yoghurt added before the meat is cooked until very tender. This is then tossed in cooked rice and garnished with coconut and currants. The garnish can be fried first.

lamb cooked in yoghurt with spices and rice

SERVES 4

25 g/1 oz/2 tbsp ghee or butter
2 large onions, thinly sliced
500 g/18 oz diced stewing lamb
5 ml/1 tsp ground ginger
1.5–2.5 ml/¼–½ tsp chilli powder
5 ml/1 tsp garam masala
2 cardamom pods
2 pieces of cinnamon stick
1 bay leaf, torn in half
2.5 ml/½ tsp salt
2.5 ml/½ tsp coarsely ground black pepper
5 ml/1 tsp grated fresh root ginger

1.5 ml/¼ tsp caraway seeds
120 ml/4 fl oz/½ cup plain yoghurt
350 g/12 oz/1½ cups basmati rice
50 g/2 oz/½ cup frozen peas (optional)
60 ml/4 tbsp currants and 60 ml/ 4 tbsp desiccated (shredded) coconut, to garnish

TO SERVE:
Popadoms, a side salad, cucumber raita (yoghurt flavoured with chopped mint and cucumber), lime pickle and mango chutney

1 Heat the ghee or butter in a saucepan. Add the onions and fry for 3–4 minutes until golden. Transfer to the crock pot.

2 Add the lamb to the saucepan and brown on all sides. Add all the spices, the bay leaf, salt, pepper, ginger and caraway seeds. Cook, stirring, for 1 minute.

3 Stir in the yoghurt, then transfer it all into the crock pot. Cover and cook on High for 4–5 hours.

4 About 20 minutes before you are ready to eat, cook the rice according to the packet directions, adding the peas, if using, for the last 5 minutes' cooking. Drain.

5 When the meat is cooked, add the cooked rice to the pot and fork through. Serve garnished with currants and desiccated coconut with popadoms, a side salad, cucumber raita, lime pickle and mango chutney.

This dish from Bangladesh, rezala, is very easy to prepare. It is quite a dry curry, so I like to serve a dhal with it as well as the rice and a salad garnish. If you don't like your curries too fiery, you can use less chilli powder than the amount I have given – or you could always use more if that is your preference!

braised beef in yoghurt
with chilli and cardamom

SERVES 4

75 g/3 oz/⅓ cup ghee or butter
2 onions, sliced
1 large garlic clove, crushed
700 g/1½ lb braising steak, cubed
3 bay leaves
7.5 ml/1½ tsp chilli powder
1 piece of cinnamon stick
4 cardamom pods
1.5 ml/¼ tsp ground cloves

5 ml/1 tsp caster (superfine) sugar
5 ml/1 tsp salt
350 ml/12 fl oz/1½ cups thick plain
　yoghurt
Wedges of lemon and a little salad,
　to garnish

TO SERVE:
Plain boiled rice and Spiced Lentils
　(see page 113)

1　Heat the ghee or butter in a saucepan. Add the onions and garlic and fry, stirring, for 2 minutes. Add the beef and continue to fry, turning and stirring, until the beef is browned all over. Tip into the crock pot.

2　Add all the remaining ingredients to the pan and bring to the boil, stirring. Tip into the crock pot, stir, cover and cook on High for 5–6 hours until the meat is really tender.

3　Remove the lid, if necessary, and continue to cook for about 30 minutes to thicken the sauce so the fat floats to the surface.

4　Discard the bay leaves, cinnamon stick and cardamom pods, if preferred, before serving with rice and dhal and garnished with wedges of lemon and little salad.

Pork is eaten by non-Muslims, especially in southern parts of India such as Goa, where this rich, fiery speciality – sorpotel – comes from. It traditionally uses malt vinegar but I like the mellow flavour of balsamic condiment better. Pigs' liver adds an exciting depth of flavour but you could omit it and use more pork and button mushrooms instead.

goan sharp and sweet spiced pork and liver stew

SERVES 4

30 ml/2 tbsp sunflower oil
2 large onions, chopped
2 large garlic cloves, crushed
2–4 dried red chillies, seeded and crushed
5 ml/1 tsp grated fresh root ginger
5 ml/1 tsp ground turmeric
1.5 ml/¼ tsp ground cloves
5 ml/1 tsp ground cumin
5 ml/1 tsp ground coriander (cilantro)
15 ml/1 tbsp garam masala
350 g/12 oz pork fillet, trimmed and cut into thick slices

350 g/12 oz pig's liver, trimmed and cut into chunks
5 ml/1 tsp salt
60 ml/4 tbsp ground almonds
150 ml/¼ pt/⅔ cup water
45 ml/3 tbsp balsamic condiment
30 ml/2 tbsp chopped fresh coriander and wedges of lemon, to garnish

TO SERVE:
Plain boiled rice and a mixed salad

1 Heat the oil in a saucepan. Add the onions and garlic and fry, stirring, for 2 minutes. Add all the spices and stir for 30 seconds.

2 Add the pork and liver and fry, stirring, for 2–3 minutes until browned all over. Stir in the salt and ground almonds. Tip into the crock pot.

3 Add the water and vinegar to the pan and bring to the boil, scraping up any sediment. Tip into the crock pot. Cover and cook on High for 2–3 hours.

4 Stir the stew, taste and re-season, if necessary. The meats should be bathed in a rich sauce. Garnish with the chopped coriander and wedges of lemon and serve with rice and a mixed salad.

This recipe for avyal comes from Kerala in Southern India. It is very versatile as it can be served as an accompaniment to dry meat curries or biryanis, or made into a complete vegetarian meal with the addition of two large cans of drained chick peas. You can vary the vegetables used according to what you have at the time.

mixed vegetable curry

SERVES 4

25 g/1 oz/2 tbsp ghee or butter
1 large onion, chopped
1 large garlic clove, crushed
10 ml/2 tsp cumin seeds
5 ml/1 tsp ground turmeric
15 ml/1 tbsp garam masala
175 g/6 oz creamed coconut
30 ml/2 tbsp tomato purée (paste)
600 ml/1 pt/2½ cups water
5 ml/1 tsp salt
Juice of 1 lime

1 large carrot, sliced
1 aubergine (eggplant), diced
1 green (bell) pepper, diced
1 red pepper, diced
1 large potato, diced
1 small head of cauliflower, cut into florets
100 g/4 oz thawed frozen green beans
1 bay leaf

1   Heat the ghee or butter in a saucepan. Add the onion and garlic and fry, stirring, for 2 minutes.

2   Add all the spices and fry for 30 seconds, then stir in the creamed coconut, tomatoe purée and water. Bring to the boil, stirring, until the coconut has melted. Stir in the salt and lime juice.

3   Put all the vegetables in the crock pot and pour the sauce over. Add the bay leaf, cover and cook on High for 3–4 hours until the vegetables are tender.

4   Taste the curry and re-season, if necessary. Discard the bay leaf before serving.

Serve this dahl with any curry as a lovely, moist accompaniment. It's particularly good if you're using a small amount of leftover meat in the main curry as lentils are high in protein. Turn it into tarka dhal *by frying 30 ml/2 tbsp of sunflower oil with 5 ml/1 tsp each of cumin and black mustard seeds until they start to pop. Drizzle the mixture over.*

spiced lentils

SERVES 4

175 g/6 oz/1 cup red lentils
1 onion, chopped
1 large garlic clove, crushed
15 ml/1 tbsp ground turmeric
15 ml/1 tbsp ground cumin
15 ml/1 tbsp ground coriander
  (cilantro)

10 ml/2 tsp paprika
450 ml/¾ pt/2 cups boiling
  vegetable stock, made with
  1 stock cube
Salt and freshly ground black pepper

1 Put all the ingredients in the crock pot. Stir thoroughly, cover and cook on High for 1½–2 hours until pulpy and most of the liquid has been absorbed.

2 Stir thoroughly, taste and re-season, if necessary.

SLOW COOKER TIP
The crock pot makes a great place to warm speciality breads such as naans. Wrap them in foil and place them in the pot. Cover and cook on High for about 15 minutes or until you need them, turning the parcel over once.

A TASTE OF THE
FAR EAST

Throughout this region food is not just about eating and enjoying food — it's an art form! Traditional Thai methods of cooking were stewing and baking or grilling; it was only as China influenced the country that stir-frying became more popular. On that note, you won't find much deep-fried food in Chinese households either. This, like some Indian dishes we eat here, was introduced to please Western palates. Peoples of the Far East are not obsessed with eating healthily — they just do! They use mainly fresh ingredients and often buy live seafood and meats. They also choose fresh fruit and vegetables from markets, using only a few preserved items such as salt fish and some pickled vegetables and dried fruits. Rice and noodles, in many forms, are the staples of the area.

Foods vary from the very bland to the spicy, with Thai curries being famous for their heat. They have adapted many Indian recipes, substituting coconut oil for ghee and coconut milk for dairy products and use herbs, such as lemon grass and kafir lime leaves, to temper the fire. In China very few dairy products are used, but soya milk and tofu figure large instead. Japanese food is probably the healthiest of all, being delicate and fresh and with very little fat. Japan's minimalist approach to design is true of its food too. Presentation is beautiful but uncluttered: flavours are simple and balanced but sensational.

This thin but delicious broth makes a lovely change from the more cloying chicken and sweetcorn soup that you so often find on the menu in Chinese restaurants. But, talking of sweetcorn, you could add a small can of corn and/or a couple of handfuls of cooked, peeled prawns (shrimp) to the soup for the last 10 minutes before serving for added luxury.

chinese chicken and mushroom soup

SERVES 4

1 chicken portion
1 onion, washed and quartered but not peeled
1 thick slice of fresh root ginger
1 celery stick, halved
1 bay leaf

900 ml/1½ pts/3¾ cups boiling chicken stock, made with 1 stock cube
100 g/4 oz shiitake or button mushrooms, sliced
30 ml/2 tbsp soy sauce
45 ml/3 tbsp dry sherry

1 Place all the ingredients except the mushrooms, soy sauce and sherry in the crock pot. Cover and cook on High for 3–4 hours.

2 Remove the chicken, onion, ginger, celery and bay leaf, leaving just the stock in the pot.

3 Discard the skin from the chicken, cut all the meat off the bones, chop and return to the stock. Add the mushrooms, soy sauce and sherry. Cover and cook on High for a further 30 minutes.

4 Ladle into bowls and serve very hot.

Red-cooked simply means cooked in soy sauce. In this Malaysian dish the lamb is steeped in soy sauce and cooked to tender perfection with Chinese five-spice powder, red peppers and a little fresh ginger to give a gloriously rich flavour. Thai fragrant rice has a wonderfully delicate taste and a soft texture.

red-cooked lamb
with thai fragrant rice

SERVES 4

700 g/1½ lb diced stewing lamb
2 large garlic cloves, crushed
1 bunch of spring onions (scallions), chopped
2 red (bell) peppers, diced
2.5 cm/1 in piece of fresh root ginger, grated
5 ml/1 tsp Chinese five-spice powder
15 ml/1 tbsp tomato purée (paste)

30 ml/2 tbsp dry sherry
75 ml/5 tbsp soy sauce
150 ml/¼ pt/⅔ cup boiling lamb stock, made with 1 stock cube
50 g/2 oz/¼ cup light brown sugar
30 ml/2 tbsp cornflour (cornstarch)
30 ml/2 tbsp water
225 g/8 oz/1 cup Thai fragrant rice
A pinch of salt

1   Put the lamb, garlic, spring onions and half the diced pepper in the crock pot.

2   Mix together the remaining ingredients except the rice, salt and the remaining pepper and pour over. Stir well, cover and cook on High for 4–5 hours.

3   If necessary, remove the lid and cook for a further 20–30 minutes to reduce the liquid to a rich, thick sauce. Alternatively, tip the juices into a saucepan and boil rapidly until thickened and reduced.

4   Meanwhile, rinse the rice well. Bring 350 ml/12 fl oz/1⅓ cups of water to the boil with the salt. Add the rice, stir, turn down the heat, cover and cook gently for 20 minutes. Turn off the heat and leave undisturbed for 5 minutes.

5   Fluff up the rice with a fork. Spoon into bowls and top with the lamb. Garnish with the reserved diced pepper before serving.

This is usually cooked on a trivet in the oven for a long time. In the slow cooker, the meat remains meltingly moist and tender and you simply crisp up the skin at the end of cooking, though you could omit this and discard the skin – a much healthier option! The skimmed cooking stock can be used as a base for a Chinese-style soup with some sliced mushrooms.

peking duck
with steamed pancakes

SERVES 6

1 small oven-ready ducking or half a
   large duck, about 1.5 kg/3 lb
30 ml/2 tbsp soy sauce
2.5 cm/1 in piece of fresh root
   ginger, sliced
1 onion, sliced
1 garlic clove, chopped
5 ml/1 tsp Chinese five-spice
   powder
15 ml/1 tbsp clear honey

150 ml/¼ pt/⅔ cup water
Sunflower oil for frying

FOR THE PANCAKES:
12 Chinese pancakes
Hoisin sauce
1 bunch of spring onions (scallions),
   cut into short, thin strips
¼ cucumber, cut into short, thin
   strips

1   Remove any excess fat from body cavity of the duck. Prick the skin all over with a fork, then rub all over with half the soy sauce. Place in the crock pot.

2   Blend together all the remaining ingredients except the oil in a saucepan. Bring to the boil, stirring, then pour over the duck. Cover and cook on High for 4–5 hours.

3   Lift the duck out of the pot and place on a plate. Carefully peel off the skin and, if you want to crisp it to serve with the flesh, dry it on kitchen paper (paper towel). Heat about 1 cm/½ in oil in a frying pan, add the skin and fry until crisp. Drain on kitchen paper, then cut into small pieces.

4   Pull all the meat off the carcass – it should fall off easily. Discard the bones, then shred the meat between two forks.

5   Warm the pancakes according to the packet directions. Smear each with a little hoisin sauce, then add some meat and crispy skin, if using, a little spring onion and some cucumber. Roll up and eat with your fingers.

Spare ribs are as popular in China as they are in the West. The meat will melt in the mouth after long, slow cooking in a crock pot. Lining the crock pot with non-stick baking parchment stops the ribs sticking to the pot (and makes for easier cleaning) but it isn't essential. You can cook half the quantity perfectly successfully even in a large pot.

chinese-style
spare ribs

SERVES 4

45 ml/3 tbsp sunflower oil
5 ml/1 tsp sesame oil
10 ml/2 tsp grated fresh root ginger
45 ml/3 tbsp clear honey
10 ml/2 tsp Chinese five-spice
 powder

2 garlic cloves, crushed
1.5 ml/¼ tsp chilli powder
90 ml/6 tbsp soy sauce
1 kg/2¼ lb Chinese short spare ribs

1 Mix 15 ml/1 tbsp of the sunflower oil with the remaining ingredients except the ribs in a large, shallow dish. Add the ribs and toss well with the hands to coat. Leave to marinate for several hours or overnight.

2 Line the crock pot with non-stick baking parchment. Heat the remaining oil in a frying pan, lift the ribs out of the marinade and fry quickly on all sides to brown. Arrange the ribs in the pot in an even layer and trickle any remaining marinade over. Cover and cook on High for 4–5 hours, turning and rearranging once or twice during cooking.

3 Lift the ribs out of the pot with tongs and serve hot.

You could make your own red curry paste from scratch but I find the pastes sold in jars are extremely good. There are numerous versions of this simple curry, but this is my favourite. Some Thai curries use more expensive steak and are quickly cooked but I find this crock pot method makes a curry with the most succulent, tender meat and a divine flavour.

thai red beef curry
with fragrant rice

SERVES 4

30 ml/2 tbsp sunflower oil
2 garlic cloves, crushed
1 onion, roughly chopped
700 g/1½ lb braising beef, cut into
    large cubes
2 large potatoes, peeled and cut into
    fairly large chunks
45 ml/3 tbsp Thai red curry paste
5 ml/1 tsp caster (superfine) sugar
1 x 400 g/14 oz/large can of
    coconut milk

Salt and freshly ground black pepper
2 red chillies, halved lengthways and
    seeded, if preferred
50 g/2 oz/½ cup raw cashew nuts
4 tomatoes, quartered
A few coriander (cilantro) leaves and
    wedges of lime, to garnish

TO SERVE:
Thai fragrant rice

1 Heat the oil in a pan. Add the garlic, onion and beef and cook, stirring and turning, for about 3 minutes until the meat is browned all over. Transfer to the crock pot and add the potatoes.

2 Blend the curry paste with the sugar and coconut milk in the pan. Season to taste and add the chillies. Bring to the boil and pour over the meat. Cover and cook on High for 5–6 hours.

3 Add the nuts and tomatoes, pushing them down well into the sauce, cover and cook for a further 30 minutes.

4 Serve spooned over Thai fragrant rice in bowls and garnish each bowl with a few coriander leaves and a wedge of lime.

Again, you could make your own green paste, but the bought versions are convenient and very good. This is also rich and delicious made with duck, in which case make sure you let the dish stand for about 20 minutes after cooking, then you can easily spoon off the excess fat before serving.

thai green chicken curry with noodles

SERVES 4

1 bunch of spring onions (scallions)
45 ml/3 tbsp sunflower oil
1 x 1.25 kg/2½ lb small chicken, cut into 8 pieces (or 4 chicken portions, halved)
60 ml/4 tbsp Thai green curry paste
1 green (bell) pepper, diced
1 x 400 g/14 oz/large can of coconut milk

1 stalk of lemon grass, finely chopped
2 kafir lime leaves
15 ml/1 tbsp Thai fish sauce
Salt and white pepper

TO SERVE:
Egg noodles

1 Trim the spring onions. Finely chop one and reserve for garnish and cut the rest into short lengths.

2 Heat the oil in a frying pan, add the chicken and brown on all sides. Transfer to the crock pot.

3 Add the spring onions and curry paste to the pan and fry for 1 minute, stirring. Add all the remaining ingredients, bring to the boil, then pour over the chicken. Cover and cook on High for 2 hours.

4 Taste the curry and re-season, if necessary. Serve spooned over egg noodles in bowls and garnish each with the chopped spring onion.

If you think sweet and sour pork has to be crispy fried battered pork balls in a sticky goo, think again. This has all the wonderful flavours of the Far East in one pot. It is a mixture of tender pork pieces, colourful vegetables and pineapple, bathed in a slightly thickened tangy sauce. You could serve Chinese egg noodles or fried rice as a change from plain.

sweet and sour pork with beansprouts

SERVES 4

30 ml/2 tbsp sunflower oil
450 g/1 lb lean pork, diced
1 garlic clove, crushed
5 ml/1 tsp paprika
1.5 ml/¼ tsp chilli powder
1 x 225 g/8 oz/small can of pineapple pieces, drained, reserving the juice
90 ml/6 tbsp soy sauce
120 ml/4 fl oz/½ cup chicken stock, made with ½ stock cube
10 ml/2 tsp clear honey
2 carrots, cut into matchsticks

2 onions, halved and sliced
1 red (bell) pepper, cut into thin strips
50 g/2 oz oyster mushrooms, sliced
5 cm/2 in piece of cucumber, cut into matchsticks
100 g/4 oz/2 cups beansprouts
30 ml/2 tbsp tomato ketchup (catsup)
30 ml/2 tbsp cornflour (cornstarch)
60 ml/4 tbsp water

TO SERVE:
Plain boiled rice

1 Heat the oil in a saucepan, add the pork and fry quickly on all sides to brown. Transfer to the crock pot.

2 Put the garlic, spices, pineapple juice, soy sauce, stock and honey in the pan. Bring to the boil, then pour over the pork. Cover and cook on High for 2 hours.

3 Add the pineapple pieces and all the vegetables except the cucumber and beansprouts to the pot. Stir, cover and cook for a further 1–2 hours until the pork is really tender.

4 Stir in the cucumber, beansprouts and ketchup. Blend the cornflour with the water, stir in, then cover and cook for a further 15 minutes.

5 Serve in bowls, spooned over rice.

Another old favourite of mine but you can't beat it for authenticity of flavour. You can buy black bean sauce in any supermarket. It has a strong, slightly salty flavour so don't add too much! The chilli oil garnish adds an extra depth of flavour but, if you don't like the spice, add some finely snipped chives to the oil instead.

chinese chicken
in black bean sauce

SERVES 4

20 ml/4 tsp cornflour (cornstarch)
30 ml/2 tbsp black bean sauce
1 large garlic clove, crushed
2.5 cm/1 in piece of fresh root
   ginger, grated
60 ml/4 tbsp soy sauce
60 ml/4 tbsp medium-dry sherry
30 ml/2 tbsp clear honey
4 skinless chicken breasts, cut into
   large chunks
100 g/4 oz shiitake or button
   mushrooms, thickly sliced

200 ml/7 fl oz/scant 1 cup boiling
   chicken stock, made with 1 stock
   cube
5 ml/1 tsp chilli powder
15 ml/1 tbsp sunflower oil
5 cm/2 in piece of cucumber, finely
   chopped, to garnish

TO SERVE:
Plain boiled rice

1   Mix together the cornflour, bean sauce, garlic, ginger, soy sauce, sherry and honey in a shallow dish. Add the chicken and turn in the marinade to coat. Cover and leave for 1 hour or overnight.

2   Spread out the chicken and marinade in the crock pot and add the mushrooms. Pour the boiling stock over, stir well, cover and cook on High for 2–3 hours.

3   Mix the chilli powder with the oil until well blended. Spoon the chicken mixture over rice, trickle the chilli oil over and sprinkle with the cucumber before serving.

Bamboo shoots add crunch to contrast with the soft texture of the chicken.
The wonderful thing is that, even with the long slow cooking in the crock
pot, they don't lose their 'bite'! Pak choi is also known as bok choy. Its
slightly mustardy flavour makes it a delicious addition to many oriental
stir-fries, soups, salads and noodle and meat dishes.

chinese chicken with bamboo shoots and pak choi

SERVES 4

4 skinless chicken breasts, cut into
  chunks
15 ml/1 tbsp dry sherry
5 ml/1 tsp light brown sugar
1 bunch of spring onions (scallions),
  diagonally sliced
175 g/6 oz button mushrooms,
  quartered
225 g/8 oz/1 small can of bamboo
  shoots, drained

150 ml/¼ pt/⅔ cup boiling chicken
  stock, made with 1 stock cube
15 ml/1 tbsp soy sauce
2 slabs of Chinese egg noodles
15 ml/1 tbsp cornflour (cornstarch)
15 ml/1 tbsp water
2 heads of pak choi, shredded

1   Place the chicken in a shallow dish. Add the sherry and sugar and mix with the hands until well coated. Cover and leave to marinate for 2 hours or overnight.

2   Put the chicken in the crock pot with the spring onions, mushrooms and bamboo shoots. Add the boiling stock and soy sauce, cover and cook on High for 2–3 hours.

3   Just before you are ready to serve, cook the noodles according to the packet directions. Drain in a colander.

4   Mix the cornflour with the water in a small cup and stir into the pot. Add the pak choi. Cover and cook for a further 30 minutes until thickened and the pak choi is almost tender but still a bit 'crunchy'. Stir in the noodles. Spoon into warm bowls and serve.

This delicious Chinese fish recipe is just as tasty when made with sea bream or red snapper. If you can be bothered, cut the carrots into pretty shapes using a petit four cutter. When I was served this dish, the fish was simply cut into four chunks, bones and all, but I prefer to fillet it for serving.

whole marinated sea bass on oriental vegetables

SERVES 4

5 ml/1 tsp grated fresh root ginger
1 garlic clove, crushed
15 ml/1 tbsp soy sauce
15 ml/1 tbsp dry sherry
10 ml/2 tsp clear honey
15 ml/1 tbsp lemon juice
1 sea bass, about 1 kg/2¼ lb, cleaned
15 ml/1 tbsp sunflower oil
5 ml/1 tsp sesame oil
3 carrots, thinly sliced
6 shiitake mushrooms, sliced

2 courgettes (zucchini), cut into matchsticks
1 red (bell) pepper, cut into thin strips
1 bunch of spring onions (scallions), cut into short lengths
150 ml/¼ pt/⅔ cup boiling chicken or fish stock, made with ½ stock cube
3 slabs of Chinese egg noodles

1   Mix together the ginger, garlic, soy sauce, sherry, honey and lemon juice in a shallow dish, large enough to take the fish. Add the fish, turn over in the marinade and leave to marinate for 2 hours, turning occasionally.

2   Heat the oils in a frying pan. Add the carrots, mushrooms, courgettes, pepper strips and about three-quarters of the spring onion (reserving the rest for garnish). Fry, stirring, for 2 minutes. Transfer to the crock pot.

3   Lay the fish on top of the vegetables, tip any marinade over and add the boiling stock. Cover and cook on Low for 2–3 hours.

4   Just before you are ready to serve, cook the noodles according to the packet directions. Drain well.

5   Carefully lift the fish out of the pot. Pour the cooking liquid into a saucepan and boil rapidly to reduce slightly. Add the noodles to the vegetables and toss.

6   Fillet the fish and cut it into four pieces. Pile the vegetables and noodles on to four warm plates, top with the fish and spoon the reduced cooking juices over. Finely chop the reserved spring onion and sprinkle over.

This Japanese stew, known as niku jaga, *needs very little preparation and is so simple but so delicious. Try experimenting with other vegetables. If you can buy the Japanese winter radish, it is lovely sliced and used instead of the diced turnip. You'll find sliced pink pickled ginger in most large supermarkets, next to the sushi or with other speciality ingredients.*

japanese braised beef and vegetable with pickled ginger

SERVES 4

700 g/1½ lb lean braising steak, cut into strips
1 bunch of spring onions (scallions), cut into short lengths
2 large carrots, diced
2 turnips, diced
100 g/4 oz button mushrooms, thickly sliced
2 potatoes, diced
150 ml/¼ pt/⅔ cup beef stock, made with ½ stock cube

75 ml/5 tbsp saké or dry white wine
40 g/1½ oz/3 tbsp light brown sugar
30 ml/2 tbsp soy sauce
A good pinch of salt
100 g/4 oz mangetout (snow peas)
20 ml/4 tsp pink pickled ginger, to garnish

TO SERVE:
Soba noodles

1   Put all the ingredients except the mangetout in the crock pot. Cover and cook on High for 4–5 hours.

2   Add the mangetout, cover and cook for a further 1 hour.

3   Taste the stew and add more soy sauce, if liked. Serve spooned over soba noodles in bowls and garnish with a little pink pickled ginger on top of each bowl.

This is so different from the usual creamy variety. The dried fruit and slow cooking gives a rich caramel colour. The sauce is a cheat, of course, but the result is similar to the original! If you have a large crock pot, put the ingredients in a 1.2 litre/2 pt/5 cup ovenproof dish inside the crock pot, with enough boiling water to come half-way up the sides of the dish.

korean rice pudding
with cherry sauce

SERVES 4

50 g/2 oz/½ cup rice flakes
120 ml/4 fl oz/½ cup boiling water
3 eggs
50 g/2 oz/¼ cup unrefined caster
   (superfine) sugar
5 ml/1 tsp natural vanilla essence
   (extract)
A good pinch of salt

450 ml/¾ pt/2 cups full-cream milk
1.5 ml/¼ tsp ground cinnamon
50 g/2 oz/⅓ cup raisins or currants
A little butter for greasing

TO SERVE:
1 x 300 g/11 oz/medium can of
   cherry pie filling, warmed

1   Mix the rice flakes with the boiling water and leave to stand for 5 minutes.

2   Beat in the eggs, sugar, vanilla and salt.

3   Bring the milk to the boil with the cinnamon added. Pour into the rice, stir well and add the raisins or currants.

4   Lightly grease the crock pot with butter. Pour in the rice mixture, cover and cook on Low for 8–10 hours until set and a deep caramel colour.

5   Serve with the warm cherry pie filling spooned over.

A TASTE OF THE
PACIFIC RIM

Australia's culinary traditions are diverse. The indigenous people created masterpieces using local seafood and freshwater fish, kangaroo, fruits, plants, nuts and berries and damper – unleavened bread baked amongst the coals of an open fire, which is still commonly eaten today. Some traditional foods spring from the British immigrants who descended on the country in 1836 – such delights as steak and kidney pie and syrup pudding are still handed down through families. But other peoples came to this large, abundant land: Italians, Greeks, Asians, South Africans and Germans to name but a few. They all brought their own cultures, foods and traditions with them, making Australia a wonderful amalgam of the world's cuisines. You'll find fusion food at its best here, along with some of the most memorable barbies ever!

All seafood is fabulous around coastal Australia. You can, of course, substitute any fish that is available to you as long as you choose a varied selection. This is really a cheat version because I use raw mixed seafood cocktail as the base. You could buy all the different seafood separately, which would be fantastic.

sydney mixed seafood chowder

SERVES 4–6

400 g/14 oz thawed frozen raw
  seafood cocktail
1 x 150 g/5 oz tuna steak, cubed
1 x 150 g/5 oz piece of cod loin or
  monkfish
25 g/1 oz/2 tbsp butter
1 onion, chopped
1 garlic clove, crushed
1 leek, thinly sliced
1 carrot, very thinly sliced
1 celery stick, chopped

1 potato, diced
1 x 400 g/14 oz/large can of
  chopped tomatoes
15 ml/1 tbsp tomato purée (paste)
750 ml/1¼ pt/3 cups fish stock,
  made with 1 stock cube
150 ml/¼ pt/⅔ cup dry white wine
1 bay leaf
A few drops of Tabasco sauce
Salt and freshly ground black pepper

1 Put all the seafood in the crock pot.

2 Melt the butter in a saucepan. Add all the vegetables and fry gently, stirring, for 5 minutes until they are softened but not browned.

3 Add the chopped tomatoes, tomato purée, stock and wine. Bring to the boil, then pour over the seafood. Add the bay leaf, a few drops of Tabasco and some salt and pepper. Cover and cook on Low for 1–2 hours.

4 Discard the bay leaf and serve very hot.

As well as making a gorgeous al fresco lunch, this would also serve eight as a small starter. If you are lucky enough to find larger squid, prepare one per person in the same way and cook for 3–4 hours for a magnificent meal. Make sure you have plenty of crusty bread to hand to mop up all the lovely juices, which are far too good to waste!

butterflied squid
in chilli sauce

SERVES 4

450 g/1 lb baby squid, cleaned and
   split open, tentacles chopped
60 ml/4 tbsp sunflower or peanut
   (groundnut) oil
2 red chillies, seeded and chopped
1 onion, finely chopped
5 ml/1 tsp grated fresh root ginger
2.5 ml/½ tsp ground cumin

5 ml/1 tsp tamarind paste
90 ml/6 tbsp boiling water
5 ml/1 tsp light brown sugar
Salt and freshly ground black pepper
5 ml/1 tsp chopped fresh basil
15 ml/1 tbsp chopped fresh parsley

TO SERVE:
Crusty bread and a crisp green salad

1 Lay the opened out squid in the crock pot.

2 Blend together all the remaining ingredients except the basil and parsley. Pour over the squid, cover and cook on Low for 2–3 hours.

3 Sprinkle with the chopped herbs and serve with crusty bread to mop up the juices and a crisp green salad.

The slow cooker is the perfect receptacle for cooking whole fish as it just doesn't dry out. Use the rest of the Australian sparkling wine to drink chilled with your meal – though, as this dish serves four, you may well need to open a second bottle! If you have a small cooker, you may only be able to cook two fish.

poached salmon trout in sparkling wine and cream sauce

SERVES 4

4 thick pieces of salmon fillet
120 ml/4 fl oz/½ cup Australian
   sparkling Chardonnay
15 ml/1 tbsp brandy
75 ml/5 tbsp water
1 bouquet garni sachet
5 white peppercorns
50 g/2 oz/¼ cup unsalted (sweet)
   butter

60 ml/4 tbsp double (heavy) cream
Salt
1 x 50 g/2 oz/small jar of red
   salmon caviare
A few stalks of flatleaf parsley

TO SERVE:
Baby new potatoes and mangetout
   (snow peas)

1   Place the fish in the crock pot. Place the wine, brandy, water, bouquet garni and peppercorns in a saucepan, bring to the boil, then pour over the fish. Cover and cook on Low for 1 hour.

2   Carefully pour off the cooking liquid into a saucepan. Cover the crock pot so the fish stays warm.

3   Boil the cooking liquid rapidly for 5 minutes until reduced and syrupy. Whisk in the butter, a little at a time, until the sauce is thickened and glossy. Whisk in the cream and season to taste with salt.

4   Transfer the fish to warm plates. Spoon a little sauce over each and top with the caviare. Garnish with parsley and serve hot with baby new potatoes and mangetout.

What could be more Australian? And yes, they do use kangaroo tail there – but oxtail works equally well! I like to think the dish has British origins and that the recipe was taken to Australia by the first immigrants, who had to adapt using kangaroo instead of the oxtail they had used back home. A flight of fancy, but it makes a nice story!

mock kangaroo tail stew in beer

SERVES 4

30 ml/2 tbsp sunflower oil
2 onions, chopped
2 celery sticks, sliced
2 large carrots, sliced
2 turnips, cut into chunks
¼ pumpkin, peeled and flesh cut into chunks
4 potatoes, cut into quarters
1 kg/2¼ lb oxtail, chopped

45 ml/3 tbsp plain (all-purpose) flour
450 ml/¾ pt/2 cups beef stock, made with 1 stock cube
300 ml/½ pt/1¼ cups lager
1 bay leaf
2.5 ml/½ tsp dried thyme
Salt and freshly ground black pepper
Chopped fresh parsley, to garnish

1 Heat the oil in a frying pan, add the onions and celery and fry for 2 minutes. Transfer to the crock pot with a draining spoon. Add all the remaining vegetables to the pot.

2 Fry the oxtail in the frying pan on all sides to brown well. Transfer to the crock pot with a draining spoon.

3 Stir the flour into the juices in the pan, then blend in the stock and lager. Bring to the boil, stirring. Pour over the meat and add the bay leaf, thyme and some salt and pepper. Cover and cook on High for 6–7 hours.

4 Discard the bay leaf. If preferred, lift out the pieces of oxtail, take all the meat off the bones and return the meat to the stew. Taste and re-season, if necessary. Stir and serve hot sprinkled with parsley.

This has its roots in Vietnam, where it is quite a fiery dish. Here the flavour is mild and subtle, perfect to enjoy with a chilled 'tinnie'! If you like spicier food, try adding one or two seeded and chopped fresh green chillies to the sauce; the result will be fabulous. For added elegance, you could sprinkle the dish with whole cashews instead of the chopped peanuts.

yellow creamy coconut chicken

SERVES 4

30 ml/2 tbsp sunflower oil
1 bunch of spring onions (scallions), finely chopped
2 garlic cloves, finely chopped
450 g/1 lb boned skinless chicken thighs, cut into pieces
10 ml/2 tsp ground turmeric
5 ml/1 tsp ground ginger
5 ml/1 tsp ground cumin
1 stalk of lemon grass, finely chopped

100 g/4 oz creamed coconut
300 ml/½ pt/1¼ cups water
Salt and freshly ground black pepper
45 ml/3 tbsp single (light) cream
50 g/2 oz/½ cup roasted peanuts, chopped
A handful of torn fresh coriander (cilantro) leaves

TO SERVE:
Plain boiled rice

1 Heat the oil in a pan, add the spring onions, garlic and chicken and fry, stirring, for 3 minutes. Tip into the crock pot.

2 Add the spices to the pan with the creamed coconut and water. Bring to the boil, stirring, until the coconut has melted. Tip over the chicken and season well. Cover and cook on High for 2–3 hours.

3 Stir in the cream, taste and re-season, if necessary. Serve over rice, sprinkled with the chopped peanuts and torn coriander leaves.

Slow cooking the ribs first before finishing them on the barbecue or under the grill makes them so meltingly tender that the meat simply falls off the bones when you eat them and removes every hint of fattiness. Take care not to burn them on the fierce heat of the coals, because they have a high sugar content.

barbecued sticky lamb spare ribs

SERVES 4

1.25 kg/2½ lb whole breast of lamb
60 ml/4 tbsp red wine vinegar
45 ml/3 tbsp clear honey
30 ml/2 tbsp tomato ketchup
(catsup)

15 ml/1 tbsp tomato purée (paste)
15 ml/1 tbsp Worcestershire sauce
15 ml/1 tbsp soy sauce
A few drops of Tabasco sauce
1 garlic clove, crushed

1   Trim as much fat from the lamb as possible with a large, sharp knife, cutting between each bone to separate the breast into spare ribs.

2   Place the pieces in the crock pot and cover with boiling water. Add half the vinegar. Cover and cook on High for 3–4 hours until really tender.

3   Mix together all the remaining ingredients, including the remaining vinegar, in a shallow dish. Drain the lamb, add to the dish and turn over each rib until they are well coated in the sauce.

4   Barbecue or grill (broil) for about 8 minutes, turning once or twice and basting occasionally, until stickily glazed and a rich dark brown.

This can either be served straight from the crock pot or thrown on the barbie at the end to crisp and brown. If finishing it over the coals, cook the chicken for about 1¹/₂ hours only, then transfer to the barbecue for about 15 minutes until cooked through and browned. If you cook it completely in the crock pot first, it may fall apart as it will be so tender.

aussie barbecued chicken pot

SERVES 4

4 chicken portions
1 garlic clove, crushed
Juice of ½ lemon
5 ml/1 tsp clear honey
10 ml/2 tsp tomato purée (paste)
1.5 ml/¼ tsp chilli powder
1.5 ml/½ tsp ground cumin
1 onion, very thinly sliced

2 carrots, coarsely grated
2 courgettes (zucchini), coarsely grated
Salt and freshly ground black pepper
120 ml/4 fl oz/½ cup cider or apple juice

TO SERVE:
Wild rice mix

1   Lay the chicken in a shallow dish. Mix together the garlic, lemon juice, honey, tomato purée, chilli and cumin and smear all over the chicken. Leave in a cool place to marinate for at least 2 hours.

2   Put the onion, carrots and courgettes in the crock pot. Season well. Top with the chicken and pour the apple juice around. Cook on High for 2 hours.

3   Serve the vegetables and chicken on a bed of wild rice mix with the juices spooned over.

This is a historic dish! It is believed to have been cooked by some of the first free British settlers (as opposed to the convicts transported to Australia) in the 1800s. But it's likely that it was a meal for governors and other high-ranking officials rather than the ordinary folk, who were, on the whole, fairly poor.

pâté-stuffed
pot roast chicken

SERVES 4

1.25 kg/2½ lb oven-ready chicken
60 ml/4 tbsp wholemeal
  breadcrumbs
100 g/4 oz smooth liver pâté with
  garlic
45 ml/3 tbsp chopped fresh parsley
40 g/1½ oz/3 tbsp butter or
  margarine
100 g/4 oz lardons (diced bacon)
2 carrots, diced

2 leeks, sliced
450 g/1 lb baby new potatoes,
  scrubbed but left whole
300 ml/½ pt/1¼ cups boiling
  chicken stock, made with 1 stock
  cube
Salt and freshly ground black pepper
30 ml/2 tbsp cornflour (cornstarch)
30 ml/2 tbsp water

1 Wipe the chicken inside and out with kitchen paper (paper towels) and pull off any fat just inside the body cavity.

2 Mash the breadcrumbs with the pâté and 30 ml/2 tbsp of the parsley. Use to stuff the neck end of the bird and secure with cocktail sticks (toothpicks).

3 Melt the butter or margarine in a pan, add the chicken and turn to brown all over. Remove from the pan and set aside.

4 Add the lardons, carrots, leeks and potatoes to the pan and cook, stirring, for 2 minutes. Tip into the crock pot and place the chicken on top. Add the stock and some seasoning. Cover and cook on High for 3–4 hours.

5 Transfer the chicken and vegetables to a carving dish. Spoon off any excess fat from the cooking juices. Blend the cornflour with the water in a saucepan and pour in the cooking juices. Bring to the boil and cook for 1 minute, stirring. Taste and re-season, if necessary.

6 Carve the chicken and serve with the vegetables and sauce.

Pheasant is farmed extensively in Australia, so you'll often find it on the menu. This is modern fusion food, not traditional Aussie fare, but incorporates fine ingredients producing a fabulously clever blend of flavours to create a very elegant dish indeed. Use two small hen pheasants, halved, if you are big eaters.

pheasant with baby beetroot and mushrooms

SERVES 4

1 cock pheasant, quartered
60 ml/4 tbsp cornflour (cornstarch)
Salt and freshly ground black pepper
25 g/1 oz/2 tbsp butter
8 cooked baby beetroot (red beets), quartered
100 g/4 oz chestnut mushrooms, sliced
1 onion, finely chopped
2 celery sticks, finely chopped, reserving the leaves

8 juniper berries, lightly crushed
60 ml/4 tbsp port
200 ml/7 fl oz/scant 1 cup chicken stock, made with ½ stock cube
15 ml/1 tbsp brandy
10 ml/2 tsp tomato purée (paste)
2.5 ml/½ tsp dried mixed herbs
Chopped fresh parsley, to garnish

TO SERVE:
Fluffy mashed potatoes and a green salad

1 Coat the pheasant pieces in the cornflour seasoned with a little salt and pepper. Heat half the butter in a frying pan, add the pheasant and brown all over. Transfer to the crock pot and scatter the beetroot and mushrooms around.

2 Heat the remaining butter in the frying pan, add the onion and celery and cook, stirring, for 2 minutes. Add any remaining cornflour to the pan and stir in the juniper berries, port, stock, brandy and tomato purée. Bring to the boil, then pour over the pheasant. Sprinkle with the mixed herbs. Cover and cook on High for 2½–4 hours until the pheasant is tender.

3 Taste and re-season, if necessary. Sprinkle with a little chopped parsley and serve hot with fluffy mashed potatoes and a green salad.

This dish has its roots in the South Sea Islands of Fiji, Tahiti, the Cook Islands, Samoa, New Caledonia, Tonga and Vantuatu. It's a lovely sweet and sour combination that is refreshingly light. I first tried a version of it in my teens, when an old boyfriend, who was in the Merchant Navy, brought back the recipe from one of his trips.

south pacific chicken with pineapple

SERVES 4

4 chicken portions
2.5 ml/½ tsp garlic salt
Freshly ground black pepper
30 ml/2 tbsp sunflower oil
1 onion, cut into chunky wedges
2 celery sticks, thinly sliced
4 tomatoes, quartered
1 red (bell pepper), sliced
1 green pepper, sliced
1 small sweet potato, cut into small
  chunks

225 g/8 oz/1 small can of pineapple
  pieces in natural juice, drained,
  reserving the juice
15 ml/1 tbsp soy sauce
15 ml/1 tbsp cornflour (cornstarch)
30 ml/2 tbsp toasted desiccated
  (shredded) coconut, to garnish

TO SERVE:
Plain boiled rice

1 Wipe the chicken with kitchen paper (paper towels) and season with the garlic salt and some pepper. Heat the oil in a frying pan, add the chicken and brown on all sides. Transfer to the crock pot.

2 Add the onion, celery, tomatoes, sliced peppers and sweet potato to the pan and fry, stirring, for 2 minutes. Tip into the crock pot and add the pineapple pieces.

3 Make up the pineapple juice to 300 ml/½ pt/1¼ cups with water. Add to the frying pan, bring to the boil and pour over the chicken. Cover and cook on High for 3–4 hours.

4 Mix together the soy sauce and cornflour in a saucepan. Transfer the chicken and vegetables to warmed plates and pour the cooking liquid into the saucepan. Bring to the boil and cook for 1 minute, stirring. Taste and re-season, if necessary.

5 Pour the sauce over the chicken, sprinkle with the toasted coconut and serve with rice.

Blue Mountain pepper is actually the ground leaf of the mountain pepper tree, which grows in the Blue Mountain rain forest in New South Wales and other rain forests in Australia. I've used coarsely ground rainbow peppercorns instead, which add a good, peppery flavour and an attractive finish.

blue mountain peppered lamb shanks with fragrant plum chutney

SERVES 4

4 lamb shanks
30 ml/2 tbsp redcurrant jelly (clear conserve), warmed
30 ml/2 tbsp coarsely crushed rainbow peppercorns
150 ml/¼ pt/⅔ cup lamb stock, made with ½ stock cube
60 ml/4 tbsp white Chardonnay
Salt
1 large sprig of rosemary

FOR THE CHUTNEY:
2 spring onions (scallions), finely chopped

8 ripe plums, halved, stoned (pitted) and chopped
30 ml/2 tbsp white balsamic condiment
30 ml/2 tbsp plum or hoisin sauce
15 ml/1 tbsp chopped fresh rosemary
A pinch of salt
Caster (superfine) sugar, to taste
Small sprigs of rosemary, to garnish

TO SERVE:
Celeriac and potato mash, broccoli

1 Brush the shanks all over with the jelly and coat in the crushed peppercorns. Place in the crock pot.

2 Pour the stock and wine into a saucepan, bring to the boil and pour around the lamb. Season lightly with salt and add the sprig of rosemary. Cover and cook on High for 5–6 hours.

3 Meanwhile, to make the chutney, put all the ingredients in a small saucepan and simmer for about 10 minutes until pulpy. Taste – if the plums were not very ripe you may need to sweeten the chutney slightly with sugar. Tip into a small serving dish.

4 When the meat is very tender, strain the cooking liquid into a small saucepan and boil rapidly for 2–3 minutes until slightly reduced. Transfer the lamb to warm plates, spoon the juices over, garnish with sprigs of rosemary and serve with the plum chutney, celeriac and potato mash and broccoli.

Damper is a fairly dry, coarse, unleavened Aussie bread, cooked on a campfire in a billy can. But – amazingly – you can get extremely successful results when it is cooked in a crock pot, though you don't, of course, get that smoky flavour. Traditionally it is eaten hot from the pot, smeared with syrup.

crock pot australian damper bread

MAKES 1 LOAF

450 g/1 lb/4 cups self-raising flour
5 ml/1 tsp salt
50 g/2 oz/½ cup dried milk powder
  (non-fat dry milk)

1 x 330 ml can of lager or 330 ml/
  11 fl oz/scant 1⅓ cups water
A little oil or butter for greasing

TO SERVE:
Golden (light corn) syrup

1 Mix the flour and salt with the milk powder and enough of the lager or water to form a soft, slightly sticky dough.

2 Grease the crock pot with oil or butter and line the base with non-stick baking parchment. Pop the ball of dough into the pot and cook on High for 2–3 hours or the until bread is risen and spongy.

3 Serve torn into pieces with golden syrup smeared over.

SLOW COOKER TIP

You can cook baby pavlovas in a large crock pot. Line the pot with non-stick baking parchment. Make a 1 egg white quantity of meringue and spoon into four small 'nests' as far apart as possible on the paper. Cover and cook on Low for 1½ hours, then turn off the cooker and leave until the meringues are cold and have dried out. They will be more biscuit-coloured than when cooked conventionally but will taste fine. Fill with cream and fruit as usual.

INDEX